Miracles of Jesus

Lessons from the
Miraculous Power of JESUS

(Transforming Lives through Faith)

Gerard Assey

Miracles of Jesus

Lessons from the Miraculous Power of JESUS
By
Gerard Assey
© Copyright 2023 by Author

Published by:
Gerard Assey
19/18, Palli Arasan Street
Anna Nagar East
Chennai - 600 102

ISBN: 978-81-965807-6-6

Table of Contents

- ✓ Preface
- ✓ Why This Book?
- ✓ How to Use This Book and Apply the Learning's in Your Life
1. Turning Water into Wine
2. The Healing of an Official's Son
3. The Expulsion of an Evil Spirit
4. The Miraculous Healing of Peter's Mother-in-Law
5. The Evening of Healing: An Outpouring of Compassion
6. The Inaugural Miraculous Catch of Fish
7. The Healing of the Leprosy-Stricken Man
8. The Centurion's Extraordinary Faith
9. The Miraculous Healing of the Paralytic
10. The Restoration of a Withered Hand
11. A Son Restored in Nain
12. Calm in the Midst of the Storm
13. Liberating Light: Jesus and the Gerasene Demoniac- Deliverance from the Abyss
14. Renewed Hope: The Woman's Faith and Healing
15. The Divine Awakening: Jairus' Daughter's Miraculous Revival
16. Divine Illumination: Restoring Sight to the Blind-Healing Two Blind Men
17. Healing the Silent Tongue: Unleashing the Tongue of the Mute
18. Reclaimed by Faith: The Healing at Bethesda's Pool

19. Abundance in Scarcity: Jesus Feeding of the 5,000
20. Overcoming the Storms: Jesus Walks on Water
21. Jesus' Miraculous Ministry in Gennesaret- Gennesaret's Encounter with Christ
22. A Mother's Undying Faith: Healing Beyond Borders
23. Ephphatha: Unleashing the Power of Divine Healing
24. Feeding the Multitude: A Lesson in Divine Abundance
25. Restoring Sight: A Lesson in Gradual Enlightenment
26. A Journey from Darkness to Light
27. The Power of Faith Unleashed
28. Divine Tax Payment: A Coin from a Fish's Mouth
29. Liberation of the Blind and Mute Demoniac
30. The Compassionate Healing of a Crippled Woman
31. The Sabbath Healing of a Man with Dropsy
32. The Cleansing of the Ten Lepers
33. The Resurrection of Lazarus
34. The Restoration of Bartimaeus' Sight
35. The Withering of the Fig Tree
36. Healing of the High Priest's Servant's Severed Ear
37. The Second Miraculous Catch of Fish
✓ Conclusion
✓ About the Author

Preface

In a world filled with challenges and uncertainties, the timeless stories of Jesus and His miracles continue to shine as beacons of hope, faith, and boundless love. This book: **'Miracles of Jesus:** *Lessons from the Miraculous Power of JESUS'* (Transforming Lives through Faith) covering the 37 miracles of Jesus stand as a testament to His divine nature and His unending compassion for all of humanity. These stories, recorded in the Gospels, have provided solace, inspiration, and guidance to countless generations.

This book embarks on a profound journey, delving into each of these miracles, unraveling their significance, and uncovering the invaluable lessons they hold for our lives today. Through these pages, we invite you to accompany us on a transformative exploration of faith, healing, and the boundless power of love, all exemplified through the life and works of Jesus Christ.

Each chapter within this book is dedicated to a specific miracle, recounting the circumstances, the people involved, and the profound impact of Jesus' actions. We breathe life into these ancient stories, revealing their timeless relevance in our modern world. As we dissect these narratives, we discover the remarkable ability of these miracles to touch our hearts, inspire our faith, and guide us through life's trials.

The miracles of Jesus are more than just supernatural events. They offer a mirror through which we can reflect on our own lives and our journey of faith. We encounter individuals in desperate need, and we witness Jesus's unwavering compassion and unwavering love. These narratives ask us to ponder our own need for healing, our spiritual infirmities, and our longing for divine grace.

In each chapter, we reflect on the person in need of the miracle, the witnesses who observed these divine interventions, and, above all, the Lord of the miracle, Jesus Christ. We explore the intricate threads that connect these miraculous events, weaving them into a tapestry of profound spiritual teachings and wisdom that can guide us in our own lives.

The purpose of this book is not merely to recount historical events but to unearth the enduring relevance and application of these stories. By doing so, we aim to help you draw strength and inspiration from the miracles of Jesus, realizing that the same compassion, love, and miraculous power are available to each of us in our own spiritual journeys.

May this book be a source of enlightenment, a reminder of the boundless love of Jesus, and a guide on your path of faith. Let **'Miracles of Jesus:** *Lessons from the Miraculous Power of JESUS'* (Transforming Lives through Faith) serve as a beacon, illuminating the way toward a life enriched by faith, hope, and love.

Welcome to this transformative journey through the miracles of Jesus, and may your heart and soul be touched by the enduring power of His grace.

Why This Book?

In the bustling and often overwhelming landscape of life, it can be all too easy to lose sight of what truly matters. We navigate a complex world filled with challenges, demands, and uncertainties, and it's during these times that we yearn for guidance, inspiration, and unwavering hope. The miracles of Jesus provide us with just that, and this book is a testament to their enduring power.

But why this book? Why choose to delve into the stories of Jesus' miracles when the world offers a multitude of paths to explore? The answer lies in the timeless wisdom, transformative power, and boundless love that these stories embody.

A Source of Hope:

The miracles of Jesus offer a wellspring of hope in a world that often seems devoid of it. In our darkest hours, when we confront suffering, doubt, and despair, these stories remind us that we are not alone. They whisper to us that a loving Savior, who once walked the earth performing wondrous deeds, is with us even now.

The message is clear: no matter the depths of our suffering, the breadth of our doubts, or the weight of our burdens, there is a source of hope, strength, and healing available to us. This book serves as a beacon of that hope, guiding you through each miracle and its profound implications for your life.

A Message of Transformation:

These miracles offer more than mere stories of supernatural occurrences. They are potent parables, brimming with profound insights into our human experience and the transformative power of faith, love, and purpose.

As we explore these narratives, we will delve into the lives of those who came to Jesus in need. We will uncover how their afflictions and yearnings mirror our own. In their stories, we find echoes of our own struggles and victories, fears and triumphs. Through their experiences, we are presented with the opportunity to transform our lives.

A Guide for Modern Living:

The miracles of Jesus are more than historical events. They are timeless, living guides for navigating the complexities of modern existence. We will examine their lessons and explore how they resonate with the contemporary challenges we face.

Each story is a wellspring of wisdom, offering insights into how to navigate suffering, exercise faith, embrace love, and discover our purpose. In these pages, you will find not only inspiration but also practical guidance on how to apply these miracles in your daily life.

How to Use This Book and Apply the Learning's in Your Life

As you embark on this journey through the miracles of Jesus, it's essential to approach this book with intention and an open heart. Here's how you can use this book as a transformative guide and apply its profound learning's in your life:

1. Read with an Open Mind and Heart:
Approach each chapter with an open heart and a willingness to embrace the teachings embedded within these miraculous stories.

2. Reflect on Your Own Life:
As you explore each miracle, take time to reflect on your own life. Consider your struggles, doubts, and desires. How do they align with the person in need of the miracle in each story?

3. Recognize Your Witnesses:
Identify the witnesses to these miracles, as they often mirror the reactions and doubts we encounter in our own lives. Reflect on how faith and doubt manifest in your personal journey.

4. Embrace the Lessons:
Absorb the lessons offered by each miracle. Recognize that these stories are more than just historical accounts; they are guides for modern living.

5. Apply the Wisdom:
Take the wisdom found in each narrative and apply it to your life. This book serves as a practical guide, and you'll discover how these ancient stories can address contemporary challenges.

6. Daily Application:

Incorporate these lessons into your daily life. Consider how they can guide your interactions, decisions, and responses to the world around you.

7. Share the Wisdom:
The miracles of Jesus offer a profound message of love and healing. Share this wisdom with others, becoming a beacon of hope and inspiration in their lives.

8. Prayer and Contemplation:
Spend time in prayer and contemplation. As you explore each miracle, seek a deeper connection with the divine. Open your heart to the transformative power of faith and love.

9. Journal Your Journey:
Keep a journal of your reflections and experiences as you progress through this book. Document your growth, insights, and the application of these miracles in your life.

10. Be a Living Miracle:
Ultimately, recognize that you are a living miracle. Just as Jesus's miracles brought hope and healing to those in need, you have the power to extend love, compassion, and transformation to those around you.

As you read, reflect, and apply the wisdom of these miracles, you will find that they have the potential to enrich your life, deepen your faith, and empower you to face the challenges of the modern world. The miracles of Jesus are timeless beacons of hope, reminding us that we are never alone in our journey.

By opening your heart to their messages, you can discover the boundless love, hope, and healing that these stories offer.

May your journey through this book be transformative, and may you carry the lessons of these miracles with you on your path to a life of faith, love, and purpose.

Let's start this exciting journey…Now!

1. Turning Water into Wine

Scripture References: John 2:1-11

In the inaugural miracle of Jesus, we find ourselves transported to Cana, a picturesque region nestled in the heart of Galilee, within the sacred land of Israel. Here, amidst the joyous festivities of a wedding feast, Jesus made his divine debut, demonstrating his extraordinary power and benevolence.

The wedding celebrations in those days were no mere day-long affairs; they often stretched over a week. Among the esteemed guests reveling in the joy of the occasion were Jesus, his mother, Mary, and his devoted disciples. The connection between the host and the guest of honor, Jesus, remains a subject of intrigue to this day.

The festivities took an unexpected turn when the wine supply, crucial to the merriment, unexpectedly ran dry. Mary, ever watchful and compassionate, felt the need to address this crisis and approached Jesus, saying, "They have no more wine."

However, Jesus, aware of the divine timing of his miracles, replied with profound wisdom, "Woman, why do you involve me? My time has not yet come." Undeterred, Mary, in her unwavering faith, turned to the servants and instructed them, "Do whatever He tells you."

In close proximity, six large stone jars, each capable of holding between 20 to 30 gallons, traditionally designated for ceremonial purification, stood ready. Jesus, with unshakable confidence, directed the servants to fill these jars with water, instructing them to do so to the very brim.

Once the jars brimmed with water, Jesus issued the next directive: "Now take some out and give it to the master of the banquet." Obediently, the servants complied, offering the transformed liquid to the master of the banquet.

Upon sipping the contents, the master of the banquet, astounded by the taste and quality of the wine, was left in wonder. He was unaware of its miraculous origin, but the servants who had drawn the water bore witness to this extraordinary transformation. Turning to the bridegroom, the master of the ceremony marveled, "Everyone brings out the best wine first and then the cheaper wine after the guests have had too much to drink; but you have saved the best till now."

This inaugural miracle in Cana of Galilee marked the beginning of a series of signs through which Jesus revealed his divine glory, solidifying the faith of his disciples.

Reflection:
- ✓ The Person in Need of the Miracle: The bride and bridegroom, along with the joyous guests at the wedding, found themselves in need of wine to continue their celebration.
- ✓ The Witnesses to the Miracle: Mary, the mother of Jesus; his devoted disciples; the diligent servants; the joyful wedding guests; and the master of the ceremony all bore witness to this miraculous transformation.
- ✓ The Lord of the Miracle: Jesus Christ chose a wedding celebration to launch his miracles, an event symbolizing blessing, provision, and the meeting of needs. This act exemplifies his inclination to bless and provide for us,

regardless of how trivial or substantial our needs may appear.

Application/Lesson:

The story of turning water into wine offers a profound lesson: Jesus possesses the extraordinary ability to transform the good into something far superior. In our lives, he cares for our every need, whether it seems significant or trivial, turning the ordinary into the extraordinary for his glory. All we must do is surrender ourselves to his divine will, and the ordinary will become extraordinary in his capable hands.

2. The Healing of an Official's Son

Scripture References: John 4:43-54

In the chronicles of Jesus' miraculous deeds, the second revelation unfolds in a vastly different setting than the first. While the initial miracle took place amidst the jubilant atmosphere of a feast, the second miracle is cast under the somber shadow of impending death and mourning.

Within the city of Cana, there resided a royal official, burdened by the illness of his beloved son. News of Jesus' presence in Cana reached his ears, and without hesitation, he embarked on a journey to seek the divine intervention of this renowned healer. His son's condition was dire, on the brink of death, compelling the official to traverse the arduous 20-mile journey from Cana to Capernaum, beseeching Jesus to save his child.

Standing before the official, Jesus recognized the skepticism that often hindered faith. He remarked, "People won't believe in Me unless they see Me perform miracles." Nevertheless, he extended his compassionate words to the distressed father, saying, "Go your way; your son lives."

With unwavering trust in Jesus' words, the official departed on his journey homeward. Along the way, his servants intercepted him with the miraculous news that his son had not only recovered but was also in perfect health. Inquiring about the exact moment of the recovery, the servants disclosed that it had occurred around 1 PM, coinciding with the precise moment when Jesus had uttered the life-restoring words, "Your son lives."

At this revelation, the official and his entire family embraced the belief in Jesus as the Lord of their lives. In healing the official's son, Jesus revealed his divine authority, transcending the limitations of physical distance. This miracle exemplified Jesus as the sovereign Lord, unbound by the constraints of the material world.

Reflection:
- ✓ The Person in Need of the Miracle: The sick son, whose life hung in the balance, and the distressed father, who humbly placed his trust in Jesus, transcending his pride. As a result, his faith was magnified.
- ✓ The Witnesses to the Miracle: All those present at the scene, including the disciples, and the official's loyal servants, who bore witness to this transformative miracle.
- ✓ The LORD of the Miracle: Jesus Christ, whose divine power and authoritative words instilled faith and healing. His spoken word carried the weight of divine authority.

Application/Lesson:
This remarkable encounter with Jesus imparts profound lessons. It teaches us the value of humility, emphasizing the importance of placing our complete trust in Jesus, guided by his boundless compassion, power, and wisdom. The miracle not only demonstrates that Jesus' power transcends the confines of physical distance but also underscores his dominion over all creation. Through this narrative, we learn that Jesus is the Lord, unhindered by any limitations.

3. The Expulsion of an Evil Spirit

Scripture References: Mark 1:21-27, Luke 4:31-36

One day, Jesus and His devoted followers embarked on a journey to the picturesque town of Capernaum, nestled along the Galilean shores. Their visit coincided with the sacred Sabbath, a day of rest and worship for the Jews, drawing them to the synagogue to deepen their understanding of God's teachings. Little did they know that this Sabbath day would become a pivotal moment in their lives.

Within the synagogue, Jesus assumed the role of a teacher, captivating the assembly with his remarkable authority and wisdom. His teachings left the crowd in awe, for unlike previous instructors, Jesus possessed an unprecedented depth of knowledge and authenticity. It was as though he spoke with a divine authority, resonating deeply within the hearts of those who listened.

However, the atmosphere took an unsettling turn when a man, gripped by an evil spirit, suddenly cried out. The presence of this malevolent force became palpable, a sinister influence emanating from the depths of darkness.

The possessed man's voice spoke, but it was the evil spirit within him that bellowed, "What do You want with us, Jesus of Nazareth? Have You come to destroy us? I know who You are—the Holy One of God!"

Unperturbed by the menacing presence, Jesus issued a commanding warning to the evil spirit, saying, "Be quiet, and come out of him!" The very essence of Jesus' words resonated with divine authority.

In response, the evil spirit convulsed the man violently, causing him to fall to the ground, and with a final, piercing shriek, the spirit departed, leaving the man unharmed. Those who bore witness to this miraculous encounter were left astounded, whispering amongst themselves, "What is this? A new teaching—and with authority! He even gives orders to evil spirits, and they obey Him."

Never before had they witnessed such an extraordinary display of authority and power. Jesus' actions were unparalleled, confirming that He was indeed a unique and divine figure. News of this incredible incident spread like wildfire throughout Galilee, as people eagerly shared the astonishing account of Jesus' authoritative teachings and his power to command even the most malevolent of spirits.

Reflection:
- ✓ The Person in Need of the Miracle: The man tormented by a demon, suffering in the grip of darkness.
- ✓ The Witnesses to the Miracle: The congregation gathered in the synagogue, including Jesus' dedicated disciples, who stood in awe of this remarkable event.
- ✓ The LORD of the Miracle: Jesus Christ, the divine figure whose very words carried unparalleled authority and the power to exorcise evil spirits.

Application/Lesson:
The expulsion of the evil spirit vividly illustrates that even demons recognize the sovereignty of Jesus. In the face of the name of Jesus, every power must

yield, be it an evil spirit, an ailment, or any other adversity. At the mere mention of His name, these forces must flee, bowing before His supreme authority. The lesson is clear: in Jesus, we find the ultimate power and protection, and through Him, we can triumph over the darkest of challenges.

4. The Miraculous Healing of Peter's Mother-in-Law

Scripture References: Mathew 8:14-15, Mark 1:29-31, Luke 4:38-39

Following the remarkable events at the synagogue in Capernaum, Jesus, accompanied by his devoted disciples, returned to the residence of Simon Peter. This unassuming home served as the backdrop for an extraordinary demonstration of Jesus' compassion and power.

Within the confines of this humble abode lay Simon's mother-in-law, confined to her bed by a debilitating fever of alarming severity. Her condition invoked great concern among those present, and they wasted no time in bringing the matter to Jesus' attention. It was a testament to the faith and trust they placed in His divine abilities.

Moved by their plea, Jesus approached the ailing woman. With a gentle and reassuring touch, He grasped her hand and tenderly helped her to her feet. The transformation was immediate and astonishing. As if by the mere contact of His hand, the fever that had tormented her vanished, and she rose from her bed with newfound strength and vigor.

What followed was a beautiful act of gratitude. With renewed vitality, she proceeded to prepare a meal for Jesus and his disciples. The impact of this miraculous healing rippled through the room, filling it with a sense of awe and wonder.

Reflection:
- ✓ The Person in Need of the Miracle: Peter's mother-in-law, who lay bedridden, gripped by a high fever, in need of divine intervention.
- ✓ The Witnesses to the Miracle: Peter and the believers who shared a bond of friendship with him, their hearts brimming with faith.
- ✓ The LORD of the Miracle: Jesus Christ, the embodiment of compassion and divine power, whose touch and presence could bring miraculous healing.

Application/Lesson:

This miraculous account speaks profoundly to us. It underscores that when we surrender our lives to Jesus, He not only assumes responsibility for our well-being but also extends His grace and care to our entire family. Through a single act of compassion and healing, Jesus was not only able to restore Peter's family but also ushered in a sense of renewal throughout the entire town. This story reminds us that Jesus can work through us to bring blessings to others. Just as Peter's mother-in-law became a means of service and gratitude, we too can be instruments of His grace, impacting the lives of those around us.

5. The Evening of Healing: An Outpouring of Compassion

Scripture References: Matthew 8:16-17, Mark 1:32-34, Luke 4:40-41

Following the miraculous healing of Peter's mother-in-law, the atmosphere in Capernaum was electric, charged with the anticipation of more extraordinary wonders. At sunset, the people of the town flocked to Jesus, bearing with them the burden of various afflictions. The evening was set to become a canvas on which Jesus would paint the profound tapestry of His divine compassion.

In a display of boundless love and unwavering compassion, Jesus laid His healing hands on each person, one by one, embracing their diverse afflictions. In His presence, their suffering was transformed into hope, their pain into relief. The healing touch of Jesus knew no bounds; it embraced all who sought solace.

Furthermore, many in the crowd were tormented by malevolent spirits, who, with voices full of fear, cried out, "You are the Son of God!" However, Jesus, the Messiah, did not desire the testimonies of these malevolent spirits. Their intentions were malicious and ulterior, meant to subvert the divine mission of Christ.

The battle for human souls was in full swing. Each of Christ's miracles was a powerful statement, a declaration of His divine nature and authority as the Son of God. These wonders underscored the depth of His love and His unwavering commitment to the salvation of humanity.

Reflection:
- ✓ The Persons in Need of the Miracle: All those who gathered that evening, encompassing the sick and those oppressed by malevolent forces.
- ✓ The Witnesses to the Miracle: The multitude of people who encircled Jesus, bearing witness to His profound acts of compassion.
- ✓ The LORD of the Miracle: Jesus Christ, the epitome of divine grace and power.

Application/Lesson:
The evening of healing, marked by Jesus' compassionate touch, serves as a reminder that His supernatural acts of love and power drew people toward Him, revealing His divine nature and opening hearts to the message of salvation. In these miraculous displays, Jesus demonstrated not only His authority over nature but also His limitless compassion.

These acts bore testimony to His unwavering love, echoing through time to assure us that the One whose heart has been set on us from the beginning of time will go to any extent to see us restored to wholeness and blessed. In Jesus, we find a compassionate Savior, and in His miracles, we discover the proof of His love, pointing us towards the path of salvation and healing.

6. The Inaugural Miraculous Catch of Fish

Scripture References: Luke 5:1-11

On a day like no other, Jesus stood beside the glistening waters of the Lake of Gennesaret, known also as the 'Sea of Galilee.' As a crowd fervently gathered around Him, hanging on His every word, He stood at the epicenter of a place where many of His miraculous works would unfold.

The shores were adorned with two fishing boats, temporarily abandoned by their weary owners engaged in the laborious task of washing their nets. Seizing an opportunity, Jesus entered one of the boats, specifically Simon's, and requested that it be pushed out a short distance from the shore. From this unique pulpit, Jesus began to teach the eager masses who had assembled to hear His words.

After imparting His wisdom and teachings to the multitude, Jesus turned His attention to Simon, saying, "Put out into deep water, and let down the nets for a catch." Simon, an experienced fisherman who had toiled tirelessly throughout the night without success, responded with humility and trust, saying, "Master, we've worked hard all night and haven't caught anything. But because you say so, I will let down the nets."

Despite their expertise and knowledge of the best fishing practices, they chose to act on Jesus' command, even though it defied conventional wisdom. Their obedience was soon rewarded with a miraculous harvest of fish so vast that their nets began to strain and tear.

Quickly, they signaled their companions in the other boat for assistance. The combined haul was so immense that both vessels were on the verge of sinking beneath the weight of their astonishing catch. Overwhelmed by this extraordinary event, Simon Peter fell at Jesus' feet, recognizing the divine presence in their midst. He declared, "Go away from me, Lord; I am a sinful man."

This miracle transcended the ordinary; it resonated with an extraordinary power that left all in awe, including James and John, the sons of Zebedee, who were Simon's partners in the fishing business.

In response to Simon's profound recognition of his own unworthiness, Jesus assured him, "Don't be afraid; from now on, you will fish for people." This marked the beginning of a relationship that would culminate with another miraculous catch of fish, symbolizing Simon's new role as a shepherd of souls.

Reflection:

- ✓ The Person in Need of the Miracle: Peter, his boat, his nets, his toil throughout the night, and most importantly, his faith.
- ✓ The Witnesses to the Miracle: The multitudes who had gathered eagerly to hear Jesus' teachings.
- ✓ The LORD of the Miracle: Jesus Christ, whose authority and power led to a profound transformation and promotion.

Application/Lesson:

This story invites us to offer not only our boats and nets but our very souls to Jesus. Surrendering our lives to His guidance allows Him to take the helm and steer us toward extraordinary possibilities. "It is no longer I who live, but Christ lives in me."

Many people grapple with life's challenges, striving to accomplish everything through their own strength. Yet, when we invite God into every aspect of our lives, our efforts are amplified, and our potential is limitless. As the miraculous catch of fish demonstrated, God's guidance and authority can yield blessings that far surpass our human capabilities, ensuring that we sail through life's challenges with divine purpose and abundance.

7. The Healing of the Leprosy-Stricken Man

Scripture References: Matthew 8:1-4, Mark 1:40-45, Luke 5:12-14

Descending from the sacred heights after delivering the transformative "Sermon on the Mount," Jesus found Himself surrounded by a multitude of followers. Among the crowd, a man afflicted by the dreaded curse of leprosy approached the Savior. He knelt at Jesus' feet, his face pressed to the ground, and implored with unwavering faith, "If you are willing, you can make me clean."

Leprosy, in those days, was not only a crippling physical ailment but a societal scourge, regarded as a divine punishment. Those afflicted were cast out of the cities, banished to live in isolation with others similarly afflicted, and were mandated to maintain a six-foot distance from the healthy. The disease had ravaged this man's entire body, leaving no part unscarred.

Yet, in the face of this affliction, Jesus was not repelled. His heart brimmed with compassion, and He responded, "I want to; be healed." With that, He reached out and touched the leper, instantly dispelling the disease that had plagued him for so long.

Ordinarily, mere contact with a leper would result in contamination, but not with Jesus. His touch brought healing, not infection. The man's affliction vanished in an instant.

Having restored the leper's physical well-being, Jesus issued a stern instruction: "See that you don't

tell this to anyone. But go, show yourself to the priest and offer the sacrifices that Moses commanded for your cleansing, as a testimony to them."
The man's elation, however, overcame his restraint, and he eagerly spread the news to everyone he encountered. As a consequence, Jesus was compelled to stay outside the towns in solitary places, as people from all corners continued to seek Him.

Reflection:
- ✓ The Person in Need of the Miracle: The leper, desperate and in need, who directed his faith toward Jesus.
- ✓ The Witnesses to the Miracle: Jesus' disciples and the surrounding crowd, who observed this wondrous transformation.
- ✓ The LORD of the Miracle: Jesus Christ, whose spontaneous and immediate compassion extended to all in need, regardless of their condition.

Application/Lesson:
The touch of the Master's hand did more than just heal the body of a rejected beggar; it transformed him into a new person, restored to the fold of humanity. This miracle is a poignant reminder of the incredible grace of God, capable of mending the broken and reconciling sinners to God.
Christ's touch holds the power to enable individuals to do good, speak words of kindness, perceive the needs of others, hear the encouraging voice of God, and journey to places requiring spiritual nourishment. The story encapsulates the profound and transformative effect of Christ's touch, offering

redemption, healing, and a renewed sense of purpose to all who seek Him.

8. The Centurion's Extraordinary Faith

Scripture References: Matthew 8:5-13, Luke 7:1-10

As Jesus arrived in the town of Capernaum, a centurion, a high-ranking Roman officer, approached Him with a plea. His servant, someone very dear to him, lay on the precipice of death, paralyzed and suffering excruciatingly. The centurion, displaying his compassion and humility, made an earnest request to Jesus, saying, "Lord, my servant lies at home, paralyzed, suffering terribly."

Jesus, ever the epitome of compassion, promptly offered to go and heal the ailing servant. His response was immediate: "Shall I come and heal him?"

The centurion, however, astounded Jesus with his unwavering faith. He replied, "Lord, I do not deserve to have you come under my roof. But just say the word, and my servant will be healed. For I myself am a man under authority, with soldiers under me. I tell this one, 'Go,' and he goes; and that one, 'Come,' and he comes. I say to my servant, 'Do this,' and he does it."

In that moment, Jesus marveled at the centurion's extraordinary faith and shared with His disciples that He had not found such faith, even in the land of Israel. Recognizing the centurion's profound faith and humility, Jesus responded, "Go! Let it be done just as you believed it would." With that declaration, the centurion's servant was healed instantaneously.

This story exemplifies Jesus as the living Savior, capable of performing miracles both then and now, for He remains unchanging throughout all time.

Reflection:
- ✓ The Person in Need of the Miracle: The ailing servant, unable to approach Jesus due to paralysis, and the centurion, a compassionate and humble man who believed in the authority of Jesus' word. His faith was remarkable, as he trusted that his servant would be healed with a mere word.
- ✓ The Witnesses to the Miracle: The Jewish elders, the disciples, and the gathered crowd, all of whom observed this extraordinary demonstration of faith.
- ✓ The LORD of the Miracle: Jesus Christ, revealing His humility, promptness, power, and admiration for the centurion's faith.

Application/Lesson:
In the homes of many proud individuals, Jesus entered, but their hearts remained closed to His blessings. However, in the case of the centurion, Jesus did not enter his house physically; instead, He entered his heart, met his needs, and extended His blessings. This account underscores the significance of humility. It teaches us that true humility opens the door for Jesus to enter our lives, fulfill our needs, and bless us.

9. The Miraculous Healing of the Paralytic

Scripture References: Matthew 9:1-8, Mark 2:1-12, Luke 5:17-26

In the bustling town of Capernaum, word of Jesus had spread like wildfire. People from all corners gathered to witness His extraordinary presence and teachings. The house where Jesus stayed was encircled by a vast crowd, with every inch occupied, both inside and out.

As Jesus addressed the eager congregation, a remarkable incident unfolded. Four men, gripped by unwavering faith, were determined to bring a paralyzed man before the Savior. Unable to penetrate the dense throng, they concocted an ingenious plan. With sheer determination, they ascended the roof and, through their own labor, created an opening. Lowering the paralytic, who lay on a mat, right before Jesus, they demonstrated their faith in action.

In the face of this extraordinary display of faith, Jesus, deeply moved, looked upon the paralyzed man and declared, "Get up, take your mat and go home." In an instant, the man who had been bound by paralysis for so long rose to his feet, lifted his mat, and walked out before the amazed crowd. Their voices rang with awe as they declared, "We have never seen anything like this."

Reflection:

- ✓ The Person in Need of the Miracle: The paralytic, a man robbed of the ability to live life

to the fullest. He had life, but his paralysis had confined him to a limited existence.
- ✓ The Witnesses to the Miracle: Simon Peter, the homeowner, Jesus' disciples, the four men who carried the paralytic, the scribes, and the guests in Peter's house. Their eyes beheld this wondrous event.
- ✓ The LORD of the Miracle: Jesus Christ, whose heart was deeply touched by their extraordinary faith. Before physical healing, He addressed the man's spiritual well-being, emphasizing His concern for our souls.

Application/Lesson:

This remarkable story urges us to be agents of love and persistence as we endeavor to bring our friends and relatives, who may be spiritually paralyzed, into the presence of Jesus. Just as the four men overcame obstacles to reach Jesus, we, too, may encounter challenges along the way. However, our faith should motivate us, for faith is a force that moves mountains and is always rewarded.

Jesus' compassion and power continue to mend the spiritual paralysis that afflicts so many. He reminds us that before physical healing, it is our spiritual condition that matters most. This story serves as an enduring testament to the boundless mercy and life-altering grace of our Savior.

10. The Restoration of a Withered Hand

Scripture References: Matthew 12:9-14, Mark 3:1-6, Luke 6:6-11

Once again, it was the sacred Sabbath day, and Jesus entered a synagogue, where a man with a withered and shriveled hand sought solace. The sanctity of the Sabbath forbade any work, and certain onlookers, perhaps mischief-makers, observed with keen interest, anticipating whether Jesus would heal this man.

Jesus, always perceptive, was aware of their scrutiny and posed a question, "Is it lawful to heal on the Sabbath?" With unshakable wisdom, He continued, "If any of you has a sheep and it falls into a pit on the Sabbath, will you not take hold of it and lift it out? How much more valuable is a person than a sheep! Therefore, it is lawful to do good on the Sabbath."

Heeding the compassionate call within Him, Jesus turned to the afflicted man and said, "Stretch out your hand." In obedience, the man extended his withered hand, and before the eyes of all present, it was made whole, as perfect as the other hand.

In response, the mischief-makers departed, their hearts hardened, as they plotted against Jesus.

Reflection:
- ✓ The Person in Need of the Miracle: The man with the withered right hand, a symbol of his ability to work, greet others, and give and receive. He demonstrated not only his ailment but also faith, obedience, and courage, which ultimately led to his miraculous restoration.

✓ The Witnesses to the Miracle: The Jewish elders, who were often bound by legalistic interpretations, prioritizing the letter of the law over its compassionate spirit. It is under grace that man finds peace, whereas the law tends to instill fear.
✓ The LORD of the Miracle: Jesus Christ, the sole possessor of the power to achieve the impossible and bring about profound transformation.

Application/Lesson:
This narrative underscores the inseparable link between faith and obedience. True faith is always accompanied by a willingness to obey, even when confronted with challenges or social norms. Jesus not only restored the man's physical capability but also rekindled his ability to do good, reminding us that our faith should manifest in acts of kindness and compassion. In this story, Jesus shows us that under grace, hearts are liberated, and healing is not bound by rigid laws but is an expression of divine love and mercy.

11. A Son Restored in Nain

Scripture References: Luke 7:11-17

Journeying with His disciples and a multitude of followers, Jesus ventured into the quaint village of Nain, nestled near the town of Capernaum. As they approached the village gate, a somber procession unfolded before their eyes. A deceased young man, the sole son of a widow, was being carried out to his final resting place, accompanied by a sorrowful crowd from the village.

The moment Jesus beheld this heart-wrenching scene, His compassion flowed forth. With words of solace, He gently said to the grieving mother, "Don't cry." Moved by deep empathy, He stepped forward and touched the bier that bore the lifeless young man. In a voice imbued with divine authority, Jesus uttered, "Young man, I say to you, get up!" Miraculously, the deceased youth sat up and began to speak, and Jesus restored him to his astonished mother.

The onlookers were filled with awe and promptly acknowledged the divine presence among them. They proclaimed, "A great prophet has appeared among us; God has come to help His people." The remarkable news of Jesus' compassionate act of resurrection quickly spread throughout Judea and the surrounding regions.

This heartwarming account exemplifies the boundless love that extends even to the most destitute and bereaved, transforming profound grief into overwhelming joy.

Reflection:

- ✓ The Person in Need of the Miracle: The widow, who had endured the loss of her husband and now faced the devastating loss of her only son, her last source of hope. She had been left with nothing, and her world was shattered.
- ✓ The Witnesses to the Miracle: Jesus' disciples, the crowd that accompanied Him, and the bystanders, all of whom were privileged to witness this extraordinary event.
- ✓ The LORD of the Miracle: Jesus Christ, the One who transforms the direst of circumstances. He is the Restorer of life, capable of calling into existence things that did not exist (Romans 4:17).

Application/Lesson:

No matter the depth of our spiritual despair, Christ raises us with Him to bestow the gift of eternal life. This poignant story underscores the truth that in Jesus, we find hope, restoration, and transformation. His love knows no bounds and extends even to the darkest corners of our lives, illuminating them with His radiant grace.

12. Calm in the Midst of the Storm

Scripture References: Matthew 8:23-27, Mark 4:35-41, Luke 8:22-25

Following a long and strenuous day filled with preaching, teaching, and healing the multitude that flocked around Him on the western shore near Capernaum, evening approached, and Jesus, weary from His labors, sought respite. In His fatigue, He directed His disciples to embark on a journey across the lake to the other side, a mountainous region, where He could find rest. With His disciples onboard, they set out on the peaceful waters, while the gentle evening tranquility enveloped them.

Amidst this serene backdrop, Jesus, exhausted, quickly fell into a deep slumber. However, suddenly and without warning, a violent storm of extraordinary severity swept over the lake. Waves surged, the boat was tossed violently, and the disciples, seasoned fishermen, found themselves confronted by a tempest unlike any they had encountered before. Fear gripped their hearts, as they faced the real and imminent threat of drowning.

In their desperation, the disciples awoke their sleeping Lord, their voices laden with fear, "Lord, save us! We're going to drown!" With a commanding presence, Jesus roused from His sleep and, rebuking the tempest, declared, "You of little faith, why are you so afraid?" To the raging elements, He issued a calm yet authoritative command, "Peace! Be still!" In an instant, the wind ceased, and a profound calm descended upon the sea.

In the aftermath of this extraordinary event, the disciples were left in awe, pondering amongst themselves, "Who then is this, that even the wind and the sea obey Him?"

Reflection:
- ✓ The Persons in Need of the Miracle: The disciples, symbolizing those who encounter the storms of life, whether in the form of fear, sadness, anger, doubt, or guilt.
- ✓ The Witnesses to the Miracle: We all bear witness to the storms that assail us in life. These storms can take various forms, but they all have the potential to disturb our peace.
- ✓ The LORD of the Miracle: Jesus Christ, whose unshakable authority and command over the elements of nature serve as a reminder that He is not perturbed by our pleas but by our lack of faith.

Application/Lesson:
The words "Peace, be still" not only calmed the tempestuous sea but serve as a reminder that God's Word can rebuke any storm in our lives. Jesus' unwavering mastery over the elements highlights His ability to bring peace to the storms that buffet us. This account demonstrates the power of faith and serves as a profound illustration of how Jesus brings calm in the midst of life's most turbulent moments.

13. Liberating Light: Jesus and the Gerasene Demoniac -Deliverance from the Abyss

Scripture References: Matthew 8:28-33, Mark 5:1-20, Luke 8:26-39

Following the awe-inspiring display of His authority over the elements, Jesus and His disciples arrived in the region of the Gerasenes, a place where an unsettling presence awaited them. There, they encountered a man tormented by a legion of demons, residing among the tombs, where he had been driven to madness, causing such violence that no one dared to pass that way.

However, as this deranged man caught sight of Jesus, a transformation occurred. Instead of aggression, he approached Jesus, bowing before Him and exclaiming, "What do you want with us, Jesus, Son of the Most High God? Have you come here to torture us before the appointed time?"

Intrigued, Jesus inquired about the demon's name. The response was chilling: "My name is Legion, for we are many." The demons, pleading not to be cast into the abyss, asked to enter a nearby herd of pigs instead. Jesus granted their request, and as they left the man, they rushed into the swine. In a chaotic frenzy, the entire herd of about 2,000 pigs stampeded off a steep bank and into the lake, where they perished.

Those who tended the pigs hastened to the nearby town to convey this astounding occurrence, including the healing of the demon-possessed man. The entire town was stirred, and they went out to meet Jesus.

Reflection:
- ✓ The Person in Need of the Miracle: The man, who had been held captive by a battalion of demons, akin to an army of 6,000 soldiers.
- ✓ The Witnesses to the Miracle: The people in the vicinity, who, rather than rejoicing in the man's deliverance, reacted with astonishment and concern. Jesus' disciples were also present.
- ✓ The LORD of the Miracle: Jesus Christ, the liberator who came to free all from the clutches of darkness.

Application/Lesson:
Jesus always takes the first step. His heart overflows with compassion when He encounters individuals ensnared in misery, suffering, or bondage. The deliverance of the Gerasene demoniac exemplifies Jesus' boundless mercy and His desire to set everyone free. This story serves as a testament to His power and willingness to break the chains that bind us, offering liberation and salvation to all who seek it.

14. Renewed Hope: The Woman's Faith and Healing

Scripture References: Matthew 9:20-22, Mark 5:25-34, Luke 8:42-48

While conversing with Jairus, an official seeking help for his ailing daughter, Jesus found Himself amidst a bustling crowd. It was in this sea of people that an extraordinary encounter took place.

A woman, who had suffered from a debilitating and unceasing flow of blood for twelve long years, heard of Jesus. Her anguish had only deepened as she sought healing from countless doctors, exhausting her financial resources, with no sign of improvement. Yet, when she learned of Jesus' presence, she harbored a glimmer of hope that whispered, "If I but touch His clothes, I will be made well."

Summoning remarkable courage, she navigated her way through the throng surrounding Jesus and, with unwavering determination, reached out to touch the fringe of His cloak. In that very instant, her prolonged suffering ceased, and she felt a profound transformation coursing through her body.

Aware that an extraordinary power had flowed from Him, Jesus turned and inquired, "Who touched My clothes?" Astonished, Peter, one of His disciples, exclaimed, "There are so many people pressing against You, and You ask, 'Who touched Me?'" Yet, the woman, trembling in fear, stepped forward and humbly revealed her truth. She recounted her plight, confessing that her touch had miraculously restored her health.

Responding with tenderness, Jesus declared, "Daughter, your faith has made you well. Go in peace, and be healed of your disease."

Reflection:

- ✓ The Person in Need of the Miracle: This woman bore not only the physical affliction of her condition but also the psychological anguish, the ritual impurity that distanced her from family and friends, and the financial burden of fruitless medical treatments. Her faith, however, shone brilliantly.
- ✓ The Witnesses to the Miracle: Among the witnesses were Jairus, who sought healing for his daughter, the disciples, and the crowd that the woman had to traverse to reach Jesus.
- ✓ The LORD of the Miracle: Jesus Christ, renowned and powerful, possessed extraordinary knowledge and delivered three invaluable gifts to the woman: confidence, an adopted status as His daughter, and the gift of peace.

Application/Lesson:

No matter how daunting the challenge, even when others have despaired, Jesus always holds the perfect solution. He transforms valleys of despair, discouragement, and disturbance into gates of hope. All it takes is faith from our end, a touch of faith, to unlock His miraculous power and grace.

15. The Divine Awakening: Jairus' Daughter's Miraculous Revival

Scripture References: Matthew 9:18, 23-26, Mark 5:21-24, 35-43, Luke 8:40-42, 49-56

In the vibrant town of Capernaum, known for witnessing countless miracles wrought by Jesus, a remarkable event unfolded, underscoring His extraordinary power and compassion.

A poignant plea reached Jesus, emanating from the lips of a deeply distressed man. Jairus, a revered leader of the synagogue, cast himself at Jesus' feet, fervently entreating Him to accompany him home and lay His healing hands upon his critically ill, 12-year-old daughter. This dear child was his only one, and her life hung in the balance.

While en route to Jairus' home, Jesus encountered another soul in dire need. A woman, who had suffered from a debilitating flow of blood for over a dozen years, sought solace in the healing touch of the Savior. As Jesus spoke words of comfort and restoration to her, time hung heavily.

In this tense interlude, a messenger rushed to Jairus with devastating news: his beloved daughter had succumbed to her illness and passed away. Yet, Jesus' response was one of unwavering faith and compassion. He assured Jairus, "Do not fear; only believe, and she will be well."

Upon their arrival, the scene was one of grief and lamentation, with mourners filling the home. But Jesus declared, "Do not weep, for she is not dead but sleeping." As He took the child by the hand and uttered, "Child, arise," her spirit returned, and she was restored to life. Jesus advised her astonished parents to provide her with nourishment, highlighting His profound ability to resurrect the seemingly irretrievable.

Though some doubted the extraordinary act they had just witnessed, there was no denying that Jesus was more than an ordinary man. He was the Son of God, capable of the miraculous. His message was clear: What is impossible for man is only possible with God.

Reflection:

- ✓ The Person in Need of the Miracle: The young girl on the brink of death and Jairus, a devoted father seeking his daughter's salvation.
- ✓ The Witnesses to the Miracle: Jairus' extended family, friends, mourners, and the disciples undergoing their spiritual tutelage.
- ✓ The LORD of the Miracle: Jesus Christ, the epitome of love, an unwavering source of encouragement, and the restorer of life.

Application/Lesson:

"Do not be afraid; only believe." Christ, with His tender love, raises believers every day from their spiritual slumber and sins, ensuring that though they may stumble, they shall not be utterly cast down, for the Lord upholds them with His steadfast hand (Psalm 37:24).

16. Divine Illumination: Restoring Sight to the Blind- Healing Two Blind Men

Scripture References: Matthew 9:27-31

As the sun descended in the sky, casting its golden glow over the town, Jesus made His way towards Simon Peter's house, igniting hope and anticipation in the hearts of those who sought Him.

Amidst the bustling crowd, two blind men, driven by the fervor of faith and the promise of His miraculous touch, trailed Jesus, their voices rising in unison, "Have mercy on us, Son of David!" These men were well aware of Jesus' reputation, having heard of His awe-inspiring miracles that had unfurled in their midst. They recognized Him as the Son of David, acknowledging His Messianic identity.

In response, Jesus posed a question that would echo through their hearts: "Do you believe that I am able to do this?" With resolute faith, they answered, "Yes, Lord." With a gentle touch, He affirmed their faith and said, "According to your faith, let it be done to you." Instantly, their world of darkness was shattered, and light flooded their once-veiled eyes.

Despite His stern warning for them to remain silent about this miraculous restoration, their hearts overflowed with joy, and the news spread like wildfire throughout the district.

Reflection:

- ✓ The Persons in Need of the Miracle: The two blind men represented not only physical blindness but also the spiritual blindness that

veils a person's perception of sin, Christ's redemptive work, and God's enduring mercy. Their cry, "Have mercy on us, Son of David," signified a profound insight into Christ's Messianic role.
- ✓ The Witnesses to the Miracle: Among the onlookers were Jesus' disciples and the crowd that accompanied Him on His journey.
- ✓ The LORD of the Miracle: Jesus Christ, the divine healer who, in this instance, chose to restore sight through the intimate act of touch, offering a tangible connection with the Master's love.

Application/Lesson:
God communicates with us in ways that we can comprehend, illuminating our path with the radiance of His countenance. Just as Jesus dispelled the darkness of the blind men's lives with His touch, we are encouraged to open our eyes to the radiance of Christ, the light of the world. It is through faith that we are granted the gift of spiritual sight and the promise of God's boundless mercy.

17. Healing the Silent Tongue Unleashing the Tongue of the Mute

Scripture References: Matthew 9:32-34

As the sun dipped below the horizon, casting its soft golden glow, Jesus and His devoted disciples embarked on their journey. Amid the gathering dusk, a figure emerged from the shadows, carrying a man who was bound by an oppressive force that had silenced his tongue for far too long.

This man, tormented and unable to speak due to his demonic possession, was gently brought before Jesus. The oppressive grip of the demon was cast aside, and, miraculously, the man who had been rendered mute regained his voice. He began to speak, a harmonious testament to the divine healing power of Jesus.

The onlookers were awestruck, declaring with fervor, "Nothing like this has ever been seen in Israel." The miraculous restoration of the man's speech reverberated through their hearts, a resounding testament to the boundless compassion of Jesus.

Reflection:

- ✓ The Person in Need of the Miracle: A man who had been silenced by demonic possession, his voice held captive by forces beyond his control.
- ✓ The Witnesses to the Miracle: The astonished crowd that had gathered to witness this extraordinary healing and the disciples, who continued to learn under the tutelage of Jesus.
- ✓ The LORD of the Miracle: Jesus Christ, the embodiment of divine grace and the vessel

through which the impossible was made possible.

Application/Lesson:
Oppression and possession, both external and internal, are forces that can profoundly affect our physical and spiritual well-being. In the face of such challenges, Jesus remains unwavering, welcoming all who seek His healing touch. As witnessed by the liberation of the mute man's voice, Jesus continues to demonstrate His mastery over the impossible, serving as a beacon of hope for those who seek His divine intervention.

18. Reclaimed by Faith: The Healing at Bethesda's Pool

Scripture References: John 5:1-15

In the heart of Jerusalem, on the day of a sacred Jewish festival, a miracle unfolded. Amidst the revelry and anticipation of the feast, a man languished in obscurity. He had been bound by infirmity for 38 long years, each one passing without celebration or joy. Yet, when he least expected it, a feast of restoration was about to be served by the Savior himself.

As Jesus ascended to Jerusalem for this holy occasion, He came across a pool near the Sheep Gate, known as Bethesda. It was a place of refuge for many afflicted souls - the blind, the lame, and the paralyzed, all seeking solace from their sufferings.

Among them lay a man, a prisoner of sickness for almost four decades. When Jesus encountered this weary soul, He knew the depth of his suffering and asked a pivotal question: "Do you want to be made well?" The man, in his profound despair, revealed that he had no one to assist him into the pool when its waters were stirred, and others always outpaced him.

In an instant, Jesus commanded, "Rise, take up your bed and walk." Miraculously, the man was made whole, rising from his infirmity and shouldering his mat with newfound strength. However, this remarkable event took place on the Sabbath, a day of rest and healing that had been overshadowed by rigid rules.

Reflection:
- ✓ The Person in Need of the Miracle: A man who had suffered for 38 years, marred by sickness, friendless, and devoid of hope.
- ✓ The Witnesses to the Miracle: The watchful Jewish elders, who emphasized the letter of the law over the spirit, and the disciples, who observed this extraordinary act of compassion.
- ✓ The LORD of the Miracle: Jesus Christ, the compassionate Savior who observed, acknowledged, inquired, demonstrated His love, and issued the life-altering command for the man to rise and walk.

Application/Lesson:

This powerful narrative reveals profound truths: a. Illness can be linked to sin, emphasizing the importance of spiritual health. b. Healing is closely tied to repentance and faith in the finished work of Christ. c. A return to sin can lead to an even worse condition, underscoring the significance of perseverance in faith.

The miracle at the Pool of Bethesda is a poignant reminder that restoration and healing often arrive unexpectedly, inviting us to reclaim our lives through faith and a profound connection with the Savior.

19. Abundance in Scarcity: Jesus Feeding of the 5,000

Scripture References: Matthew 14:13-21, Mark 6:30-44, Luke 9:10-17, John 6:1-15

In the picturesque setting by the Sea of Galilee, a multitude had gathered, desperately seeking the presence of Jesus. Among them were the afflicted, the helpless, the demon-possessed, the infirm, the lame, the blind, the deaf, the crippled, and those thirsting for His wisdom. They yearned for His guidance and the healing touch of the Divine.

As news spread that Jesus was to embark on a sea voyage, the determined crowd made their way by land to the other side, brimming with anticipation. Following a tiring journey by boat, Jesus and His disciples arrived on the shores of the Sea of Galilee. Here, in the midst of stunning natural beauty, a remarkable scene unfolded.

While the day waned into evening, and the people were famished, their need was not solely spiritual but also physical. Concerned that they would return home hungry and exhausted, Jesus turned to His disciples and issued a compassionate command: "You give them something to eat."

Faced with the logistical challenge of providing for the thousands before them, the disciples could only produce five barley loaves and two fish offered by a young boy. Yet, they presented their meager provisions to Jesus, who then instructed the multitude to sit on the grass.

With the five loaves and two fish in hand, Jesus lifted His gaze to the heavens, offering a blessing and breaking the bread. The disciples distributed the multiplied food among the eager assembly. Astonishingly, all 5,000 men, along with their families, partook in the feast, their hunger sated, with twelve baskets left to collect the abundance that remained.

This story of abundance amid scarcity serves as a poignant testament to Jesus' unfailing care for our human needs and His unwavering dedication to ensuring that we have the provisions we require.

Reflection:

- ✓ The Person in Need of the Miracle: The 5,000 men, women, and children in the crowd, who were hungry for both spiritual nourishment and care.
- ✓ The Witnesses to the Miracle: The disciples, notably Philip and Andrew, who struggled with the limited resources, and the young boy who offered his humble offering.
- ✓ The LORD of the Miracle: Jesus Christ, the Shepherd who offers rest, the compassionate One who understands and bears the burdens of others, the Creator who can bring abundance from scarcity, and the sole source of satisfaction for the soul and heart.

Application/Lesson:

This profound narrative underscores that Jesus is acutely aware of our every need, even when we may forget to attend to ourselves. With Jesus by our side, even the most modest of provisions can multiply into an abundance. He is the Living Bread that both satisfies and strengthens, ever willing and able to meet our physical and spiritual requirements.

20. Overcoming the Storms: Jesus Walks on Water

Scripture References: Matthew 14:22-33, Mark 6:45-52, John 6:16-21

After the astounding miracle of feeding the 5,000, Jesus demonstrated His profound care for His disciples. He instructed them to embark on a boat and sail to the other side of the tempestuous Sea of Galilee, while He retired to the solitude of a mountain to pray. The disciples, seasoned fishermen familiar with the Sea of Galilee's sudden and violent storms, soon found themselves battling the elements far from the safety of the shore.

In the dead of night, the disciples struggled to keep their boat steady against the battering winds and surging waves. Fear enveloped them as the storm's ferocity rendered their expertise ineffectual. However, in their darkest hour, their Savior approached.

From the shore, Jesus observed their perilous situation and understood their dire need. With unparalleled power over nature, He stepped onto the water, walking toward His distressed disciples. His appearance struck terror into their hearts, and they cried out, thinking they beheld a ghost. Yet, Jesus tenderly assured them, "Take heart; it is I. Do not be afraid."

Peter, demonstrating a glimmer of extraordinary faith, called out, "Lord, if it is You, command me to come to You on the water." Heedless of the tempestuous sea, Jesus beckoned Peter to join Him. Stepping out of the boat, Peter miraculously walked on the water toward Jesus. But as the strength of the storm assailed his faith, fear gripped him, and he began to sink. In his desperation, he implored Jesus to save him.

Without hesitation, Jesus reached out His hand and rescued Peter, chastising him gently: "You of little faith, why did you doubt?" The moment they entered the boat, the tempest subsided. Those in the vessel, profoundly moved, worshiped Jesus, declaring, "Truly You are the Son of God."

This extraordinary narrative illustrates that God hears our prayers even from a distance, comprehending our deepest needs and rushing to our aid when we are in distress.

Reflection:

- ✓ The Person in Need of the Miracle: The disciples, notably Peter, who ventured to walk on water.
- ✓ The Witnesses to the Miracle: All the disciples, who bore witness to the calming of the storm and Peter's miraculous but brief walk on water.
- ✓ The LORD of the Miracle: Jesus Christ, who not only stilled the raging sea but also enabled Peter to perform the miraculous feat of walking on water. His actions manifest His omnipotent control over the elements.

Application/Lesson:

When the turbulent storms of life threaten to overwhelm us and our control over destiny falters, the Lord of heaven and earth walks toward us on the very waves that disturb us, commanding their cease. In the midst of life's tempests, it may not always be simple to recognize the presence of the Lord; yet, He is ever present, ready to reach out and rescue us when we cry out for help. Jesus stands as our sole refuge and Savior, regardless of the trials we face.

21. Jesus' Miraculous Ministry in Gennesaret- Gennesaret's Encounter with Christ

Scripture References: Matthew 14:34-36, Mark 6:53-56

Following the awe-inspiring event of Jesus walking on water upon the Sea of Galilee, He and His disciples reached the shores of Gennesaret. Word spread like wildfire throughout the region as the people recognized Jesus. Hastily, they dispatched messages to the surrounding countryside, announcing His presence.

In response, throngs of individuals afflicted by a myriad of illnesses and infirmities flocked to Him. Their earnest pleas resonated with desperation as they sought healing for their diverse ailments. Eager and persistent, they implored Jesus, even if it meant a mere touch of the edge of His cloak. Astonishingly, those who brushed against His garment found themselves instantaneously healed.

The sick and ailing, some carried on mats, were brought to the very place where Jesus was situated. The accounts of miraculous healings spread like wildfire, drawing crowds from all directions. Wherever Jesus ventured, be it villages, towns, or countryside, the sick were brought before Him, and, by His touch or even a mere connection with His clothing, they were made whole.

Reflection:

- ✓ The Person in Need of the Miracle: An array of individuals battling illnesses, from various walks of life and backgrounds.
- ✓ The Witnesses to the Miracle: The devoted crowds who followed Jesus, along with His disciples, who were continually learning from Him.
- ✓ The LORD of the Miracle: Jesus Christ, the great Healer and Restorer of physical and spiritual well-being.

Application/Lesson:

Faith and Belief: The people of Gennesaret exhibited unwavering faith in Jesus, believing that even a touch of His garment could bring about healing. Their faith paved the way for miracles.

The Power of Request: Their fervent requests to Jesus for healing were met with overwhelming success, demonstrating the responsiveness of Christ to earnest supplication.

Sharing the Gift: They shared their knowledge of Jesus, extending the opportunity for healing to those around them. This selfless act facilitated the well-being of many.

The Simplicity of Faith: Through their faith and touch, the people of Gennesaret showcased that even a modest connection with Jesus can yield profound results.

A Welcoming Spirit: The people of Gennesaret made Jesus and His disciples feel at home. When we invite Jesus into our hearts and lives, we open the door to countless possibilities.

In the tranquil shores of Gennesaret, we discover a poignant reminder of the transformative power of faith, fervent requests, and the abiding presence of Jesus. This chapter serves as a testament to the enduring legacy of healing, where the simplest touch can bring forth profound restoration.

22. A Mother's Undying Faith: Healing Beyond Borders

Scripture References: Matthew 5:21-28, Mark 7:24-30

Journeying to the region of Tyre, Jesus embarked on a mission that would reveal the boundless nature of His compassion and the enduring power of faith. In this narrative, we encounter a Gentile woman, a mother whose heart ached for her little daughter, possessed by a relentless demon. The fame of Jesus had reached her ears, and she was determined to seek His intervention.

This devoted mother, driven by unyielding faith, approached Jesus with humility, bowing at His feet. Her singular request was for Jesus to deliver her daughter from the torment of demon possession. However, she faced a seemingly insurmountable obstacle when Jesus initially responded, "I was sent only to the lost sheep of Israel."

But her determination knew no bounds, and she pressed on, beseeching Jesus for assistance. In response, Jesus remarked, "It is not fair to take the children's food and throw it to the dogs." Still, her unwavering faith shone through as she replied, "Yes Lord, but even the dogs eat the crumbs that fall from their master's table."

Witnessing the depth of her faith, Jesus commended her, declaring, "Woman, great is your faith! Let it be done as you wish." And with that, she returned home to find her daughter healed, with the tormenting demon vanquished.

Reflection:

✓ The Person in Need of the Miracle: A tormented young girl and her mother, whose faith remained steadfast.
✓ The Witnesses to the Miracle: The disciples, who initially sought to send the mother away.
✓ The LORD of the Miracle: Jesus Christ, who recognized the strength of the woman's faith and used this encounter to reshape the perspectives of His disciples.

Application/ Lesson:

Unwavering Faith: This story highlights the remarkable strength of a mother's faith, serving as a testament that faith, regardless of one's background, is met with divine grace and healing.

Boundless Compassion: Jesus' response to the Gentile woman revealed His unwavering compassion, demonstrating that His healing touch knows no borders.

A Lesson in Faith: The disciples, through this encounter, learned the value of faith and witnessed that it transcends societal boundaries and expectations.

Faith Rewarded: This story reinforces the principle that faith, regardless of origin or circumstance, is always rewarded.

In the narrative of the Gentile woman and her possessed daughter, we find a poignant reminder that faith transcends boundaries and expectations, serving as an unerring path to divine intervention. Here, we discover a message of hope, grace, and the transformative power of unwavering faith, heralding healing beyond borders.

23. Ephphatha: Unleashing the Power of Divine Healing

Scripture References: Mark 7:31-37

Continuing His journey through the land, Jesus ventured from Tyre to the region of Decapolis. The crowds, as always, thronged around Him, bearing a man who was both deaf and mute, yearning for the miraculous touch of the Savior. Their heartfelt plea was simple: that Jesus would place His healing hand upon the afflicted man.

In a poignant moment, Jesus took the man aside, away from the pressing crowd. What followed was a sequence of actions laden with divine significance. Jesus tenderly placed His fingers into the man's ears, and with profound compassion, He touched the man's tongue. Gazing heavenward, Jesus released a deep sigh and uttered the transformational word, "Ephphatha," signifying "Be opened!" In that instant, a miracle unfolded before their eyes – the man's ears were opened, his tongue was loosed, and he began to speak with clarity.

With great humility and instruction, Jesus commanded those who witnessed this miraculous event not to spread the word. However, their amazement and the impact of this divine act couldn't be contained. Their voices resonated with admiration, exclaiming, "He has done everything well. He even makes the deaf hear and the mute speak."

Reflection:
- ✓ The Person in Need of the Miracle: A man afflicted with deafness and muteness, akin to our separation from God due to sin.
- ✓ The Witnesses to the Miracle: The disciples and the people of Sidon who were fortunate to behold this wondrous act.
- ✓ The LORD of the Miracle: Jesus Christ, whose sequence of actions symbolizes His transformative power.

Application/ Lesson:

This miraculous event demonstrates that Jesus' healing transcends mere words. In this remarkable moment, Jesus didn't simply declare, "You can hear and speak again," but He embraced the deaf man's needs on multiple levels. He engaged physically, used touch, offered a heavenly connection, and expressed divine compassion. It wasn't just the words He spoke but the way He enacted the miracle that made it extraordinary.

In applying this lesson to our spiritual journey, we understand that like the deaf and mute man, we too were once spiritually separated from God by our sins, unable to hear His voice. Yet, in a wondrous act of divine grace, Jesus spoke to our hearts, declaring, "Be opened!" This miraculous transformation mirrors the remarkable healing of the deaf and mute man, reminding us that salvation is a truly extraordinary miracle.

Let us remain open to God and His transformative power. When we allow Christ to lead our lives, no matter how tumultuous the path may be, we can rest assured that the outcome will always be for our good. Jesus has indeed done all things well, and under His guidance, our journey is marked by hope, healing, and divine restoration.

24. Feeding the Multitude: A Lesson in Divine Abundance

Scripture References: Matthew 15:32-39, Mark 8:1-13

Jesus' journey took Him along the shores of the Sea of Galilee, leading Him to a mountain where He took His seat. As always, great crowds flocked to Him, bringing their sick, and witnessing His miraculous cures. Three days had passed, and these devoted followers had nothing to eat. Jesus, in His boundless compassion, couldn't bear to send them away hungry, fearing they might falter on their way.

Gathering His disciples, Jesus expressed His deep concern and said, "I have compassion for these people; they have already been with me for these three days and have nothing to eat. I do not want to send them away hungry, or they may faint and fall down on the way." In response, the disciples queried, "Where can we get enough bread in this remote place to feed such a large crowd?"

Undeterred by the apparent scarcity, Jesus continued, "How many loaves do you have?" The disciples disclosed, "Seven, and a few small fish." Jesus instructed the crowd to sit down on the ground. Taking the seven loaves and the fish, He offered a prayer of gratitude, then broke the bread and distributed it to the disciples for serving. Miraculously, all who partook of the food were not merely satisfied but filled to the brim. Astonishingly, seven basketfuls of remnants were collected, surpassing the original offering.

The crowd numbered four thousand men, excluding women and children. Following this miraculous feast, Jesus departed by boat to the region of Magadan.

Reflection:
- ✓ The Persons in Need of the Miracle: The hungry multitude of 4,000 men, accompanied by women and children, who had been with Jesus for three days without sustenance.
- ✓ The Witnesses to the Miracle: The disciples, those seated in the crowd, and all who bore witness to this divine provision.
- ✓ The LORD of the Miracle: Jesus Christ, whose boundless compassion led to the miraculous multiplication of the meager resources—seven loaves of bread and a few fish—to satisfy the multitude.

Application/ Lesson:
This profound miracle demonstrates not only Jesus' capacity for multiplication but also His compassion for those in need. Beyond physical nourishment, Jesus ardently desires to feed our spiritual hunger with the "bread of life"—His word. In this act, we witness that Christ's miraculous power doesn't always hinge on challenges but is often stirred by sheer compassion. His actions reveal that every provision is a gift from God, highlighting the concept that all that sustains us is directly bestowed by the divine hand.

Jesus' abundant provision of physical sustenance illuminates His role as the "Bread of Life." His compassionate and gracious nature illustrates that He is our attentive, loving, all-knowing Provider, capable of intervening in our lives regardless of the circumstances.

25. Restoring Sight: A Lesson in Gradual Enlightenment

Scripture References: Mark 8:22-26

As Jesus and His devoted disciples returned to Bethsaida, a throng of people followed in His wake. Among them were a group who approached Him, bearing a blind man, their hearts filled with hope. Their plea was simple: "Please, Master, touch this man and restore his sight."

Jesus, perceiving their heartfelt request, led the blind man away from the village. With profound compassion, He took the man's hand, a tactile reassurance of His presence and intent. What followed might have appeared peculiar to an onlooker: Jesus, in His remarkable manner, spat on the man's eyes and gently laid His hands upon them. Upon doing so, Jesus posed a question: "Do you see anything?" The blind man's response was hopeful, though not quite complete. He replied, "I see people; they look like trees walking around." His partial sight, resembling the forms of walking trees, indicated that his vision had begun to stir but had not yet fully awakened.

Undeterred, Jesus once more laid His hands upon the man's eyes, and this time, the miraculous transformation occurred. The man's eyes were fully opened, and his sight was completely restored. He could now perceive the world around him with perfect clarity.

With his vision restored, Jesus instructed the man to return home and advised him, saying, "Don't even go into the village."

Reflection:
- ✓ The Person in Need of the Miracle: The blind man, who experienced a gradual healing process, reflecting a lack of initial enthusiasm, interest in knowledge, and consequently, faith.
- ✓ The Witnesses to the Miracle: The friends who brought the blind man to Jesus, the disciples, and the surrounding crowd.
- ✓ The LORD of the Miracle: Jesus Christ, the Healer, and the Restorer of sight.

Application/ Lesson:

This miracle unveils Jesus' extraordinary patience and grace, highlighting His dedication to guiding us until our spiritual insight is fully illuminated. It illustrates His role as the One who liberates us from spiritual darkness and blindness, leading us to the marvelous light of His truth. Just as the blind man's sight was progressively restored, Jesus persists in opening our spiritual eyes, making His way and teachings clear to us. He is the One who invites us out of the darkness, guiding us along the straight path He has laid out for us.

26. A Journey from Darkness to Light

Scripture References: John 9:1-12

As Jesus continued His earthly ministry, His path led Him to a profound encounter with a man who had been blind from the day of his birth. The disciples, inquisitive about the origins of this man's suffering, approached Jesus and questioned, "Rabbi, who sinned, this man or his parents, that he was born blind?"

In response, Jesus sought to broaden their understanding and deepen their faith. He explained that neither the man nor his parents were responsible for his condition. Instead, this blindness had persisted so that the works of God might be revealed through him, and God would receive the glory. In His words, He emphasized the urgency of their mission: "As long as it is day, we must do the works of Him who sent me. Night is coming, when no one can work. While I am in the world, I am the light of the world."

With these profound words, Jesus set a spiritual stage for a miraculous transformation. He stooped down and, using a mixture of mud and saliva, anointed the blind man's eyes. Instructing him to wash in the Pool of Siloam, Jesus sent him on a transformative journey.

The blind man faithfully followed Jesus' instructions. After his encounter with the waters of Siloam, he returned home, fully seeing and bathed in the glorious light of day. Yet, this newfound sight would stir the curiosity of his neighbors and acquaintances, prompting discussions and debates.

Some wondered if he was indeed the same man they had seen begging day after day. Others contested, suggesting that he merely resembled the blind beggar they had known. Yet, the man himself, now filled with the radiant light of sight, boldly declared, "I am the man." When questioned about the miraculous transformation, he testified of the extraordinary events that had unfolded: "The man they call Jesus made some mud and put it on my eyes. He told me to go to Siloam and wash. So I went and washed, and after that, I could see."

Intrigued by this miracle, they sought to find Jesus, asking the man where He might be. However, the once-blind man could only reply, "I don't know."

Reflection:

- ✓ The Person in Need of the Miracle: The man, blind from birth, symbolizing spiritual blindness. His faith, obedience, and powerful testimony are emblematic of the transformative work of Jesus in our lives.
- ✓ The Witnesses to the Miracle: The inquisitive neighbors, the skeptical Pharisees, the man's parents, and the disciples who were part of this unfolding narrative.
- ✓ The LORD of the Miracle: Jesus Christ, who, in His boundless love, initiated the divine plan to bring glory to God through this miraculous healing.

Application/ Lesson:

This story underscores that Jesus, the Light of the World, has the power to open our spiritual eyes and guide us from the darkness of ignorance and sin to the brilliance of truth and salvation. Just as the once-blind man faithfully followed Jesus' instructions, we, too, must heed His teachings and commandments to experience a transformation from spiritual darkness to radiant light.

As Jesus proclaims, "I am the way, the truth, and the life," He becomes our Savior, Physician, Teacher, and Friend, opening our eyes to the profound and enduring truth of His love and grace.

27. The Power of Faith Unleashed

Scripture References: Matthew 17:14-20, Mark 9:14-29, Luke 9:37-43

As the sun rose on a new day, Jesus, accompanied by His closest disciples – Peter, James, and John, descended from a high mountain. The mountain's tranquility stood in stark contrast to the tumultuous scene that awaited them below.

A father, his heart heavy with despair, rushed forward from the crowd that had gathered. He fell to his knees before Jesus and, with quivering voice, made a desperate plea. His only son was afflicted by a malevolent spirit, causing him to endure violent convulsions and rendering him mute. The father implored Jesus, tears in his eyes, "Teacher, I beg you to look at my son. A spirit seizes him, and he suddenly screams; it throws him into convulsions so that he foams at the mouth. It scarcely ever leaves him and is destroying him. I begged your disciples to drive it out, but they could not."

Jesus, compassion in His eyes but frustration in His voice, addressed the crowd, saying, "You unbelieving and perverse generation, how long shall I stay with you and put up with you? Bring your son here to me."

As the boy drew near, the malevolent spirit within him reacted fiercely, hurling him to the ground in a final act of defiance. But Jesus, with divine authority, rebuked the unclean spirit, restored the boy to health, and delivered him into his father's loving arms. The crowd watched in awe as the greatness of God was revealed before their very eyes.

Afterward, His disciples, their confusion apparent, approached Jesus privately and asked, "Why couldn't we drive it out?" Jesus offered them a profound and enduring lesson on faith. He replied, "Because you have so little faith. Truly I tell you, if you have faith as small as a mustard seed, you can say to this mountain, 'Move from here to there,' and it will move. Nothing will be impossible for you."

Reflection:
- ✓ **The Person in Need of the Miracle:** A tormented boy possessed by an evil spirit, and his desperate father.
- ✓ **The Witnesses to the Miracle:** The disciples, the astonished crowd, and the father who cried out for help.
- ✓ **The LORD of the Miracle:** Jesus Christ, whose compassion and divine authority led to the boy's healing.

Application/ Lesson:
This powerful miracle illustrates the remarkable potential of faith, no matter how small it may seem. Jesus' message to His disciples remains as relevant today as it was then: even a tiny seed of faith, firmly rooted in God, can accomplish the extraordinary. With unwavering faith, we can move mountains, surmount obstacles, and conquer the seemingly impossible.

Let us remember that faith has the power to overcome doubts and challenges, guiding us through life's complexities. As we face our own trials and tribulations, may we hold fast to this invaluable lesson, believing that even the smallest seed of faith can unleash profound transformation, making the impossible possible.

28. Divine Tax Payment:
A Coin from a Fish's Mouth

Scripture References: Matthew 17:24-27

Upon arriving in Capernaum, a city beside the Sea of Galilee, tax collectors approached the Apostle Peter with an inquiry, "Doesn't your teacher pay the temple tax?" Peter, with an affirmative nod, confirmed that indeed, Jesus paid the temple tax. Upon entering their dwelling, Jesus initiated a discussion about the tax, questioning Peter, "What do you think, Peter? From whom do the kings of the earth collect duty and taxes - from their own children or from others?"

Peter, without hesitation, replied, "From others." Jesus, with a gentle smile, offered His wisdom, "Then the children are exempt. But so that we may not cause offense, go to the sea, cast a hook, take the first fish that comes up, and when you open its mouth, you will find a coin. Take that and give it to them for you and Me."

Reflection:

- ✓ The Person in Need of the Miracle: Although it may appear that Jesus needed assistance, it was Peter who was required to pay the temple tax. This story imparts several profound lessons to Peter:
1. Jesus is the Lord and Son of God, exempt from the temple tax.
2. Christ symbolically represents God's temple.
3. Jesus is the ultimate ransom, having paid the price for humanity's redemption.
- ✓ The Witnesses to the Miracle: The disciples and the tax collectors.

✓ The LORD of the Miracle: Jesus Christ, who, despite being exempt from the tax, chose to pay it not only for Himself but also for Peter. The miracle underscores His lordship over nature.

Application/ Lesson:
Peter, analogous to the coin hidden in a fish's mouth, was transformed by Christ's divine guidance. This miracle serves as an allegory for the Christian mission - as the fisherman's hook brings forth hidden treasures from the sea, Christ utilizes ordinary individuals to become fishers of men, drawing them from obscurity to purpose.

Moreover, this story underscores Christ's lordship and His fulfillment of the law. His willingness to pay the temple tax, though exempt, exemplifies His commitment to maintaining peace and preventing offense. It reminds us of His divine role as the ultimate ransom, having paid the price for our redemption.

From this miraculous account, we draw the essential lesson that even the ordinary, symbolized by the coin in the fish's mouth, can be used by Christ for extraordinary purposes. Just as the fish in the sea can yield treasures, so too can ordinary individuals become instruments of divine grace and transformation.

29. Liberation of the Blind and Mute Demoniac

Scripture References: Matthew 12:22-23, Luke 11:14-23

In the presence of a multitude, a man who had fallen victim to a malevolent demon was brought before Jesus. This tormented soul was not only gripped by the malevolent entity but was also afflicted with blindness and an inability to speak.

With unfaltering compassion, Jesus healed this afflicted man, liberating him from the oppressive shackles of the demon. In an instant, the man regained his speech and was granted the gift of sight. Such a miraculous transformation befell him that the surrounding crowd was left in awe, leading them to ask, "Can this be the Son of David?"

Reflection:
- ✓ The Person in Need of the Miracle: A man held in the thrall of a malevolent demon, who suffered from blindness and an inability to speak.
- ✓ The Witnesses to the Miracle: The disciples and the awe-struck onlookers.
- ✓ The LORD of the Miracle: Jesus Christ, the compassionate deliverer.

Application/ Lesson:

The term "Satan" essentially signifies 'adversary,' representing all that opposes the benevolence of God. Jesus, as the divine deliverer, undertakes the mission of vanquishing evil in all its manifestations.

This story exemplifies that darkness, no matter how imposing, is powerless in the presence of light.

It reinforces the profound truth that the radiant light of Christ dispels even the most profound darkness. When we embrace this light, darkness is inevitably banished from our lives, and we find solace in the triumphant power of Christ over adversity. This miraculous narrative underscores the undeniable supremacy of good over evil, signifying that with Christ, we can conquer all adversities and surmount any challenge that stands before us.

30. The Compassionate Healing of a Crippled Woman

Scripture References: Luke 13:10-17

It was a sacred Sabbath day when Jesus stood before a congregation in one of the synagogues, teaching the timeless wisdom of God. Among the worshippers, there was a woman who had borne the weight of an evil spirit's affliction for eighteen long and torturous years. This malevolent force had rendered her body contorted and unable to stand upright. Yet, when Jesus laid His eyes upon her, His compassion overflowed, and He beckoned her to draw near. With gentle authority, He spoke to her, "Woman, you are set free from your ailment."

Then, with the touch of His healing hands, she was immediately transformed. Her body, once stooped and twisted, straightened, and she began to praise the divine. However, not everyone present was filled with jubilation; the leader of the synagogue, perturbed that Jesus had performed this miraculous healing on the sacred Sabbath, admonished the gathering. He proclaimed, "There are six days for work. So come and be healed on those days, but not on the Sabbath." Jesus swiftly responded to this hypocritical admonition, pointing out the humane acts of kindness enacted toward animals on the Sabbath. He argued that if it was fitting to care for animals on this holy day, then should not this woman, a child of Abraham, who had suffered in the clutches of Satan for eighteen long years, be released from her affliction on the Sabbath?

This rebuke rendered Jesus' opponents speechless, while the congregation marveled at the miraculous deeds that had unfolded before their eyes.

Reflection:
- ✓ The Person in Need of the Miracle: A woman, trapped in a crippling condition for eighteen years, unable to stand erect. Though she did not voice her desire for healing, her presence in the synagogue was an eloquent plea for release.
- ✓ The Witnesses to the Miracle: The synagogue leader, who, distressed by the healing on the Sabbath, displayed a lack of compassion, and the disciples, along with others gathered at the synagogue.
- ✓ The LORD of the Miracle: Jesus Christ. He saw her condition, called her to Him, offered the healing touch, and courageously defended her liberation against her accusers. This narrative also illustrates Jesus' regard for women.

Application/ Lesson:
This story beautifully epitomizes the compassionate touch of Jesus extended to all souls in moments of distress. Just as He reached out to free the crippled woman from her physical bondage, His divine hand stretches forth to us now, ready to set our lives upright and usher us into a renewed and profound connection with Him. It serves as a profound reminder of Jesus' unending compassion and His willingness to heal, even on the sacred Sabbath.
Furthermore, the narrative underscores Jesus' profound knowledge of the Law of Moses, His

authority over it, and His impeccable logic in dispelling objections. His treatment of women stands as an exemplary model for others to emulate, emphasizing His regard for all of God's children.

31. The Sabbath Healing of a Man with Dropsy

Scripture References: Luke 14:1-6

On a tranquil Sabbath day, Jesus embarked on a journey to the house of a prominent Pharisee, where He was invited to partake in a meal. However, the Pharisees and lawyers closely observed His every move. In His path stood a man suffering from an abnormal and painful swelling that had afflicted his entire body. Addressing the lawyers and Pharisees in His company, Jesus posed a question, "Is it lawful to heal on the Sabbath, or not?" The room fell silent. Undeterred by the palpable tension, Jesus extended His hand to heal the afflicted man and subsequently released him from his ailment. With a note of gentle reprimand, He queried them further, "Which of you, having a son or an ox that has fallen into a well on a Sabbath day, will not immediately pull him out?" Once again, His question echoed unanswered, leaving His opponents at a loss for words.

Reflection:
- ✓ The Person in Need of the Miracle: A man afflicted with dropsy, a painful condition marked by abnormal swelling.
- ✓ The Witnesses to the Miracle: This tableau unfolded before the eyes of Jesus' disciples, the Pharisee host, legal experts, fellow Pharisees, and onlookers.
- ✓ The LORD of the Miracle: Jesus Christ.

Application/ Lesson:
This story sheds light on the consequences of unbelief—a palpable lack of compassion that results from rejecting God's loving nature. Through these acts of healing on the Sabbath, Jesus meticulously restores the human aspect of the original Sabbath institution. He reminds us of its purpose as a day of rest, rejuvenation, and joy, liberating it from the confines of Pharisaic distortion. By these merciful healings, Jesus underscores the Sabbath as a day for acts of compassion. As the Lord of the Sabbath, He dedicates it through the Spirit for the dual purpose of divine worship and the service of humanity.

His boundless compassion for human suffering mirrors His heart's compassion for sinners. With His shed blood, He can grasp the hand of the sinner, heal, and then release them into a life renewed by His grace.

32. The Cleansing of the Ten Lepers

Scripture References: Luke 14:1-6

During His journey to Jerusalem, Jesus traveled along the border that divided the lands of Samaria and Galilee. As He approached a village, He encountered a group of ten men afflicted with the loathsome disease of leprosy. These men, standing at a distance as required by the law, raised their voices in unison to implore Jesus for His mercy, crying, "Jesus, Master, have pity on us!" In response to their plea, Jesus looked upon them and issued a simple command, "Go, and show yourselves to the priests."

As the ten lepers obediently embarked on their way to present themselves to the priests, they found themselves remarkably cleansed of their affliction. However, one of the ten, a Samaritan, upon realizing the miraculous healing, reversed his course. In a grand gesture of gratitude, he prostrated himself at Jesus' feet, offering fervent praise to God.

Observing this touching display of gratitude, Jesus questioned the absence of the other nine who had been similarly healed. He inquired, "Were not all ten made clean? So where are the other nine? Has no one returned to give praise to God except this foreigner?" Concluding His response to the Samaritan, Jesus blessed him further, declaring, "Rise and go on your way; your faith has made you well."

The story underlines that the Samaritan, who not only received physical healing but also spiritual blessings, was the sole returner among the ten.

Reflection:

- ✓ The Persons in Need of the Miracle: The ten lepers, all in dire need of healing, stood at a distance from Jesus, a situation reminiscent of sinners who are spiritually distant. The narrative underscores that only one of them returned, highlighting the absence of gratitude in the remaining nine.
- ✓ The Witnesses to the Miracle: While the specific witnesses are not mentioned, it's conceivable that Jesus' disciples, who were under His tutelage, were present.
- ✓ The LORD of the Miracle: Jesus Christ, whose methods of working miracles were diverse, is the central figure.

Application/ Lesson:

This miracle conveys a poignant lesson - Jesus expects gratitude from us, a simple yet meaningful acknowledgment that is rightfully His. In His compassion, He seeks to bestow more than mere physical healing. He desires to provide spiritual nourishment that endures for a lifetime and living water that not only satisfies but overflows, quenching the spiritual thirst of others. It underscores the importance of loving the Giver more than the gift.

33. The Resurrection of Lazarus

Scripture References: John 11:1-45

In the village of Bethany, there lived a man named Lazarus, along with his two sisters, Mary and Martha. This family shared a profound love for Jesus, and their close bond with Him was unmistakable. When Lazarus fell seriously ill, the sisters sent a message to Jesus, urgently pleading, "Lord, the one whom you love is sick." Upon receiving this message, Jesus declared, "This sickness will not end in death. No, it is for God's glory so that God's Son may be glorified through it."

Despite His love for Martha, Mary, and Lazarus, Jesus made the unusual choice to remain two days longer in His current location upon hearing of Lazarus' illness. Only after this delay did He set out for Bethany. However, upon His arrival, Jesus found that Lazarus had already been dead and entombed for four days. Martha, the grieving sister, lamented that had Jesus been present, Lazarus might not have died. To this, Jesus responded, "Your brother will rise again."

Guided by the mournful procession, Jesus proceeded to the tomb of Lazarus. As He beheld the somber scene, He was deeply moved and began to weep. The tomb was a cave sealed with a stone, and Martha cautioned Jesus against opening it, noting the inevitable stench due to Lazarus being deceased for four days. Unperturbed, Jesus responded to Martha, saying, "Did I not tell you that if you believed, you would see the Glory of God?" In obedience, the stone was rolled away, and Jesus looked heavenward, offering a prayer to the Father. Then, with a resounding command, He called out, "Lazarus come out."

In astonishing compliance, Lazarus emerged from the tomb, still wrapped in burial garments. Jesus instructed those present, saying, "Unbind him, and let him go." Witnessing this remarkable event, many of the Jews who had come to console Mary believed in Jesus.

Reflection:
- ✓ The Persons in Need of the Miracle: Although Lazarus was the one who had died, it was, in fact, his sisters, Mary and Martha, who needed this miraculous intervention. The family's deep love and unwavering faith in Jesus underscore the significance of this event.
- ✓ The Witnesses to the Miracle: The disciples, those who had come to comfort the grieving sisters, as well as the Jewish leaders.
- ✓ The LORD of the Miracle: Jesus Christ, who assured, "The sickness is not unto death, but for the glory of God," revealing His ability to perceive beyond life's challenges and understand the underlying purposes. He exhibited authority over life and death, demonstrating His dual nature as a perfect man and the perfect God with complete dominion.

Application/ Lesson:
This miraculous account underscores the extraordinary power of Jesus to breathe life into situations that seem hopelessly dead. It symbolizes the transformative journey from the death of our sins

to a new life in Him, granting us freedom from the fear of physical death. Christians, in Christ, no longer need to dread death. As stated in 1 Corinthians 15:55, "Where, O death, is your victory? Where, O death is your sting?" We are blessed through Christ, and our lives should reflect God's honor, as we anticipate the day we will be with Him in Heaven.

34. The Restoration of Bartimaeus' Sight

Scripture References: Matthew 20:29-34, Mark 10:46-52, Luke 18:35-43

While Jesus, accompanied by His disciples and a large crowd, was leaving the city, a blind beggar named Bartimaeus sat by the roadside, seeking alms. Upon hearing that it was Jesus of Nazareth passing by, he cried out, "Jesus, Son of David, have mercy on me!" Although many tried to silence him, he continued to call out, "Son of David, have mercy on me!"

In response to his persistent cries, Jesus stopped and instructed those around Him to summon the blind man. They conveyed the message to Bartimaeus, "Cheer up! On your feet! He's calling you." With eagerness, Bartimaeus cast aside his coat, leapt to his feet, and approached Jesus.

Addressing him, Jesus asked, "What do you want me to do for you?" To this, the blind man responded, "Lord, I want to see." In turn, Jesus said, "Go; your faith has healed you." At that very moment, Bartimaeus received his sight and embarked on the journey, following Jesus along the road. His persistence and unwavering belief were richly rewarded.

Reflection:

- ✓ The Person in Need of the Miracle: Bartimaeus, the blind beggar, exemplified unwavering faith, persistent cries for help, and an unyielding spirit. He knew his heart's

desire, and he received not only physical sight but also newfound insight, prompting him to follow Jesus.
- ✓ The Witnesses to the Miracle: The onlookers in the crowd who initially tried to silence Bartimaeus and the disciples.
- ✓ The LORD of the Miracle: Jesus Christ, the object of Bartimaeus' fervent cries, was recognized by him as famous and compassionate. Remarkably, Jesus did not compel the blind man but kindly inquired, "What do you want me to do for you?"

Application/ Lesson:

This miracle exemplifies how Jesus stands by us when others abandon us and hears our cries for help when others try to silence us. He is our ultimate refuge and shelter. As demonstrated in Bartimaeus' story, Jesus rewards persistence and faith. He granted him the gift of sight, allowing him to see what many people with perfect physical vision could not discern – the true identity of Christ as "the Son of David," the long-anticipated Savior. This narrative serves as a reminder of Jesus' unwavering mercy and His willingness to heal and restore, both physically and spiritually.

35. The Withering of the Fig Tree

Scripture References: Matthew 21:18:22, Mark 11:12-14

One early morning, as Jesus was journeying back to the city, He experienced a deep hunger. Along the road, He spotted a fig tree and approached it with the hope of finding some fruit. However, upon closer inspection, all He found were leaves. In response, Jesus said to the tree, "May you never bear fruit again!" Instantly, the tree withered and dried up. Witnessing this extraordinary occurrence, the disciples were left in amazement, questioning how the fig tree had withered so rapidly. Jesus provided them with a profound lesson, declaring, "Truly I tell you, if you have faith and do not doubt, not only can you do what was done to the fig tree, but also you can say to this mountain, 'Go, throw yourself into the sea,' and it will be done. If you believe, you will receive whatever you ask for in prayer."

In the analogy of the fig tree, we find a reminder that our purpose on Earth is to bear fruit.

Reflection:

- ✓ The Person in Need of the Miracle: The disciples, who were in need of multiple spiritual lessons.
- ✓ The Witnesses to the Miracle: The disciples, who were left astonished.
- ✓ The LORD of the Miracle: Jesus Christ, who demonstrated His authority over various aspects of life. He exhibited justice by affording the fig tree a fair opportunity to

produce fruit, yet it failed. His long-suffering was evident in His desire for none to perish.

Application/ Lesson:
This story serves as a spiritual guide, indicating God's expectations for our lives. Just as the fig tree was given everything it needed to bear fruit, we, too, have been equipped by the Lord for fruitful lives. It emphasizes that fruitlessness eventually leads to destruction. We are reminded of our purpose on Earth, which is to bear fruit. The fig tree, adorned with lush leaves but devoid of fruit, serves as a poignant reminder that hypocrisy can lead to judgment. By reflecting on this narrative, we are encouraged to express gratitude to Jesus for providing us with all the necessary resources and grace to bear spiritual fruit. Jesus, in His boundless love, eliminates any hindrances to our growth and fruit-bearing, thus bestowing upon us the power to bear abundant fruit in our spiritual journeys.

36. Healing of the High Priest's Servant's Severed Ear

Scripture References: Luke 22:50-51

After the Passover dinner, Jesus and His disciples ascended the Mount of Olives. As Jesus engaged in prayer, His disciples, situated at a short distance, fell asleep. This had already occurred twice before, and now, as Jesus returned to find them sleeping once more, a crowd, led by Judas, one of Jesus' disciples who had turned traitor, appeared. Judas, intending to identify Jesus to those who had come to arrest Him, approached Jesus and greeted Him with a kiss. In response, Jesus addressed Judas, saying, "Judas, is it with a kiss that you are betraying the Son of Man?" Perceiving the impending danger, those with Jesus inquired, "Lord, should we strike with the sword?" One of them acted swiftly, swinging his sword and cutting off the ear of the High Priest's servant. In response, Jesus immediately admonished, "No more of this!" He then touched the injured servant's ear and miraculously healed it. Following this incident, Jesus was seized and led away to the house of the High Priest.

Reflection:

- ✓ The Person in Need of the Miracle: While it may initially seem that Malchus, the servant of the High Priest, required the miracle due to his severed ear, the primary individuals in need were Peter, who found himself torn between defending Jesus and refraining from violence, and all of us.
- ✓ The Witnesses to the Miracle: The High Priest, other Jewish leaders, the soldiers, Judas,

Peter, and the other disciples in close proximity to Jesus.
- ✓ The LORD of the Miracle: Jesus Christ - His willingness to extend forgiveness and love even in the midst of personal suffering. He demonstrated these qualities, most notably, upon the Cross.

Application/ Lesson:

Jesus performed a profound miracle by healing Malchus' ear. In the midst of His arrest, He continued to work miracles and exemplify the teachings of love. This act testifies to Jesus' love for His enemies and His impeccable goodness towards them. It also serves as a testament to His divine power and His unfailing love, even when faced with adversity. By emulating this example, we can aspire to display love and compassion, even in the face of conflict and personal challenges.

37. The Second Miraculous Catch of Fish

Scripture References: John 21:4-11

This miraculous event unfolded in the wake of Jesus' resurrection when He once again appeared to His disciples by the Sea of Galilee. Among His disciples present were Simon Peter, Thomas, Nathanael, the sons of Zebedee, and two others. Simon Peter, in a moment of resolve, declared, "I'm going out to fish," to which the others replied, "We'll go with you." Together, they embarked on a fishing expedition but found their efforts fruitless as they fished throughout the night.

At daybreak, a mysterious figure appeared on the shore, and although the disciples did not immediately recognize Him as Jesus, He called out to them, saying, "Friends, haven't you any fish?" Disheartened, they replied, "No." The enigmatic figure then offered a suggestion: "Throw your net on the right side of the boat, and you will find some." Following this advice, the disciples made a catch so abundant that they could not haul the net in because of the multitude of fish.

Upon this miraculous catch, the disciple whom Jesus loved realized the identity of the mysterious figure and exclaimed to Peter, "It is the Lord!" Peter, driven by this revelation, donned his outer garment (which he had removed) and leaped into the water. The other disciples, in the boat, carefully towed the net laden with fish, for they were near the shore, approximately a hundred yards away.

Upon reaching the shore, the disciples discovered a fire of burning coals with fish and bread. Jesus then instructed them, "Bring some of the fish you have just caught." As Simon Peter re-entered the boat and drew the net to the shore, they were astonished to find it teeming with large fish, numbering a total of 153. Remarkably, the net remained intact.

Jesus invited the disciples to join Him for breakfast, and they recognized that it was the Lord. He took the bread and the fish, distributing them to the disciples. This encounter marked the third occasion on which Jesus appeared to His disciples following His resurrection.

Reflection:
- ✓ The Person in Need of the Miracle: At the suggestion of Peter, seven disciples returned to fishing, which was their former profession.
- ✓ The Witnesses to the Miracle: All seven disciples who embarked on the fishing expedition, along with the possibility of other fishermen in the vicinity.
- ✓ The LORD of the Miracle: Jesus Christ.

Application/ Lesson:
The disciples spent an entire night engaged in fishing, toiling in vain. However, they were not alone; the watchful eyes of the Lord were upon them. In our own lives, when we encounter pain, distress, or failure, we are never isolated. The One who loves us, cares for us, and comprehends our every circumstance is ever watchful. Today, Jesus continues to labor with us and within us during every need, for He is alive, resurrected, and ever present in our lives.

Conclusion

As we reach the culmination of our journey through the **'Miracles of Jesus:** *Lessons from the Miraculous Power of JESUS'* (Transforming Lives through Faith), we find ourselves standing at the threshold of an extraordinary spiritual awakening. These stories have guided us through moments of immense suffering, boundless compassion, and unwavering faith, as they invite us to a deeper understanding of ourselves and the divine presence in our lives.

The miracles of Jesus are not merely relics of the past. They are living, breathing parables that continue to unfold in the lives of those who open their hearts to their profound messages. In each of these narratives, we have found not only miracles but also profound insights that transcend time and culture, illuminating the path toward a life filled with faith, love, and purpose.

Throughout our exploration, we've discovered that the miracles of Jesus are more than mere displays of supernatural power. They are messages of hope and assurance, testaments to the boundless love of a Savior who walks with us through every storm, calms every tempest, and heals every affliction. These miracles resonate with the timeless truth that we are never alone, and that a higher power, one of unfathomable love, stands ready to aid us through the darkest hours of our lives.

We have considered the person in need of each miracle, recognizing that we share common threads with these individuals in our own journeys. Just as they came to Jesus with their afflictions, so can we approach Him with our burdens and doubts. Our deepest needs, whether physical, emotional, or spiritual, find their answer in the compassionate heart of Christ.

We've examined the witnesses to these miracles, recognizing the diverse array of individuals who observed Jesus' divine interventions. It is through their reactions that we see reflections of our own struggles with doubt, belief, and understanding. By empathizing with these witnesses, we can better understand the role of faith in our own lives and the powerful transformation it can bring.

In every miracle, we have acknowledged the Lord of the miracle, Jesus Christ, whose love and power transcend the confines of time and space. His teachings and actions provide us with guidance, strength, and a profound source of inspiration to live lives of purpose and meaning.

Throughout this journey, we've understood that the application of these miracles in our lives goes beyond simple admiration or acknowledgement. These stories are beacons of hope, calling us to a deeper connection with our faith and a higher understanding of our own purpose. We have witnessed healing, provision, and transformation, recognizing that these very same miracles are within our grasp when we align our lives with Christ's teachings and love.

As we conclude this exploration, we are left with the assurance that the miracles of Jesus are not mere stories but living, breathing lessons that transcend time. They offer us not only the hope of miraculous intervention but also the guidance to live lives filled with compassion, faith, and love.

May the 37 miracles of Jesus continue to be a source of inspiration and strength as you navigate life's challenges and triumphs. May your faith be deepened, your heart filled with love, and your spirit be uplifted as you carry these timeless stories with you on your journey.

In closing, let us remember that just as these miracles were manifestations of divine love, you too can be a living miracle, extending love, compassion, and healing to those around you.

By carrying the lessons in your heart, may your life be forever touched by the miracles of Jesus and by sharing their wisdom; you become an instrument of grace in the lives of others.

About the Author
'GERARD ASSEY'

Gerard Assey is a Graduate in Economics, a PGD in Management (HRD) and holds a Doctorate in Leadership. Gerard holds several International Qualifications in Sales, Debt Collection, Training & Teaching, and is a 'Fellow' of the prestigious 'Institute of Sales & Marketing Management'-UK, a Certified NLP Practitioner, a 'Certified Trainer', an 'Accredited Management Teacher-Behavioral Sciences', a 'Certified Competency Facilitator', a 'Certified Management Consultant'- (the International credentials of a professional management consultant, awarded in accordance with global standards of the ICMCI); and a Certification from the University of Michigan in 'Successful Negotiation: Essential Strategies and Skills'

He is also a Member of the 'National Association of Sales Professionals' backed with several years experience in varied industries, both in India and Overseas. He also holds an 'Etiquette Consultant' Certification from the USA (by Sue Fox, Author of Best Seller: 'Business Etiquette for Dummies'. She has trained some of the top celebrities' world over). He was also a recipient of a scholarship for extensive training in Japan on 'Corporate Management for India'.

Gerard Assey is 'Founder & Chief Corporate Trainer' of the Group: **'Citius, Altius, Fortius Unlimited'**- an organization that **celebrated 20 years of Glorious Service** in 2021, focusing on 3 Core Competencies:

People. Performance. Profit; in functional areas of Sales & Marketing, HR & Organizational Development, covering Recruitment, Training & Consultancy!

Having managed organizations with large Sales Forces in India & Overseas, his specialization cover extensive areas of Sales Training (All levels - Presentation, Negotiation, Key/ Strategic Accounts Management & Managerial Skills for all sectors), Bid Proposal/ Capture Planning/ Management Trainings, Retail Sales, Customer Service & Customer Retention Programs, Training for Prevention & Collection of Debt, Self & Personal Development Programs (Time Management, Teamwork & Team Building, Business Etiquette & Personal Grooming, Leadership & Managerial Skills, People Management Skills, Train-the-Trainer etc), including preparation of Custom-designed Business Manuals for Internal (HR, Induction, and Sales etc) & External use (Instruction, User Manuals).

Gerard has successfully conducted over 6000 Trainings & Workshops (as of Oct '23) all across India, Middle East, Africa, Europe & S.E. Asia. Besides public programs conducted regularly, both in India & Overseas, he has some of the top names as clients whom he services from Single Owners to large Public & Government undertakings, covering all sectors, for their in-house needs.

His website: www.CollectionSkills.com is the only one in this part of the world to be featured in the 'Collections & Credit Risk Magazine-USA' under 'Who's Who in Training' and ranks TOP, along with other websites listed below on most search engines.

Gerard is author of 95 books already (Nov 2023),

A few of our business related books:

1. Bite-sized Bits on Commonsense Management
2. Heart to Heart on Life's Principles'
3. How to become a Successful Manager
4. The Sales Professionals' Master Workbook of S.Y.S.T.E.M.S
5. The Professional Business Email Etiquette Handbook & Guide
6. The Professional Business Video-Conferencing Etiquette Handbook & Guide
7. Professional Presentation Skills
8. Exceptional Customer Service
9. Professional Tele-Marketing Skills
10. Professional Debt Collection Skills
11. The G.R.E.A.T. Sales & Service Workbook
12. Sales Training Advantage for Results (*The Ultimate Sales Training Manual to enable you stand out as a S.T.A.R.*)
13. CEO Daily Planner & Organizer
14. The Sales Professionals' Master Daily Planner
15. The Professional Debt Collector's Master Daily Planner
16. My Daily Planner & Organizer
17. MY EMERGENCY INFORMATION RECORD (Family Emergency & Peace of Mind Planner)
18. The Ultimate Therapist & Counselors Planner and Organizer
19. Building an Ethical Workplace
20. Managing Relationships at Work
21. Managing Business Meetings Effectively
22. Effective Delegation Skills
23. Goal Setting for Success
24. B2B Selling by Email
25. Professional Business Etiquette & Grooming
26. Dining Etiquette & Table Manners
27. Effective Networking Skills
28. Grooming, Etiquette & Manners for Teens, Young Adults & Future Leaders
29. Inter-Personal Skills
30. Get Ready, Get Hired!
31. Selling in a Recession
32. Effective Receivables Management in an Economic Downturn!
33. Real Estate & Property Sales Training
34. Credit Sales & Accounts Receivable Management
35. Selling Skills for Real Estate & Property Advisors
36. Take G.R.E.A.T. C.A.R.E!

37. Spa, Salon & Health Club Selling Skills
38. Selling Travel, Holiday & MICE Services
39. Selling Skills for Spa's, Salons & Health Clubs
40. Retailing in Salons & Spas
41. Selling Holiday, Vacation, Tours & Packages
42. The Power of Sales Referrals
43. Selling Luxury
44. Technical Selling Skills
45. Financial Advisors Sales Training
46. Dealing with Burnout at Work Monopolize Your Markets
47. Selling to Affluent Customers
48. Growing up with Grace
49. Financial Selling Skills
50. *The Effective Manager's Guide: Key Skills to Thrive*
51. From Aspiring to Inspiring: A Guide for New Managers on the Rise
52. The Power of Focus
53. Selling with Integrity: Sell Like Jesus The Perfect Role Model!
54. 31 Habits of Champions: Your 31-Day Journey to Greatness
55. Rejecting Grasshopper Talk: From Grasshopper to Giant-Killer-*Defeating Giants Daily!*
56. Navigate the AI-Powered Future of Bid & Proposals: Up-Skill to Stay Relevant with Alternative Career Paths & Opportunities
57. Hiring Sales Winners
58. Present with Impact
59. Success Unlocked: *Breaking Free from Habits that Hold You Back*
60. Complaints to Cheers, Feedback to Gold: Mastering Complaints Management
61. Thriving Together: *Cultivating Diversity, Equity, and Inclusion*
62. Coaching Skills for Sales Managers
63. Soaring to Success in Business & Leadership: Swifter, Higher, Stronger!
64. From Classroom to Podium: A Student's Guide to Powerful Public Speaking & Presentation Skills
65. Developing Self-Discipline
66. The CEO's 31-Day Power Plan: Unlocking Success through Essential Traits
67. Credibility Matters

…And some of his most recent Christian Books being:

1. A Bouquet of Praises for My KING
2. Christian Jokes for the Serious Religious' Folks!
3. Jesus Healed You!
4. Praise24Ever! (also in Tamil version)
5. The 5G Network of GOD
6. Building Faith over F.E.A.R- FACE EVERYTHING AND RISE with JESUS
7. Hebrew and Greek Praise and Worship Words
8. Godly Mothers' and Grandmothers' Bible Story time for Kids!
9. Miracles of Jesus in Pictures
10. Raise your Praise all 365 Days
11. Thanking GOD with an Attitude of Gratitude
12. Meditating on the Attributes of GOD
13. Puppet Scripts
14. Alcohol Ruins, JESUS Reforms, Renews & Restores!
15. Habakkuk 2:2 Christian Daily Journal, Planner & Organizer
16. ABC of GOD's Word for Handwriting Practice
17. Daily Bible Verse Handwriting Practice (Building Godly Character & Faith through Cursive Handwriting Practice!)
18. Guiding Light: Fun & Faith-Building Bible Activities for Children
19. *Rejecting Grasshopper Talk: From Grasshopper to Giant-Killer-Defeating Giants Daily!*
20. *Teen Titans of Faith: Building Courage, Determination & Christ-like-Esteem*
21. *I AM Empowered: Unleashing Divine Power with Positive Declarations*
22. *Be A Solution Provider-From Passion to Purpose: A Biblical Guide to Being the Answer to the World!*
23. Miracles of JESUS

Besides regularly contributing to business & trade journals, including international ones such as the 'Creative Training Techniques' and the 'Sales News' of the U.S.A, He is also a member of several prestigious bodies & trade associations, having participated in many Conferences & Workshops in India & Overseas.

Prior to his last assignment of leading & managing a large MNC as head, Gerard had a 3-year stint in the Middle East as a Consultant with a leading British Consultancy Firm.

As the past 'Official Country Representative' for the International Business Award- 'THE STEVIES'-(the business world's own Oscar) for about 4 years- he ensured a few Indian companies that qualify for the same every year!

Gerard can be contacted at:

Email: training@Sales-Training.in,training@CollectionSkills.com

Websites:

www.Sales-Training.in
www.EtiquetteWorks.in
www.CollectionSkills.com
www.RetailSalesTraining.in
www.SalesTrainingIndia.com
www.ManualPreparation.com
www.TrainingWithPuppets.com
www.FirstContactAcademy.com
www.SalesAndMarketingRecruiter.com

Our TRAININGS & BOOKS that can help your team

- ✓ **Sales Effectiveness**: Selling Skills for any Sector: Service/ Logistics/ FMCG Realty/ Insurance & Finance/ Media/ SPA's, Health Clubs & Salons/ Key Account Management, Effective Negotiation Skills/ Bid & Proposal Management Skills/ Retail Sales Training: Any Sector (Auto, Jewelry, Clothing, Luxury etc)
- ✓ **Customer Service Skills**-Complaints Handling & Customer Retention
- ✓ **Debt Prevention & Collection Skills**
- ✓ **Etiquette & Grooming**
- ✓ **Leadership & Managerial Skills**
- ✓ **Self & Personal Development Skills**: Presentation Skills/ Effective Communication Skills/Business Proposal Writing Skills/ Problem Solving & Decision Making Skills/ Empowering Secretaries-The perfect PA! (For Secretaries & PA's)/ Effective Time Management/ Teamwork & Teambuilding/ P.R.I.D.E- **P**ersonal **R**esponsibility **I**n **D**elivering **E**xcellence